BECOMING
YOUR BEST

RONALD W. RICHARDSON

BECOMING
YOUR BEST

A SELF-HELP GUIDE FOR THINKING PEOPLE

Augsburg Books

Library of Congress Cataloging-in-Publication Data

Richardson, Ronald W. (Ronald Wayne), 1939-
  Becoming your best : a self-help guide for thinking people / Ronald W. Richardson.
    p. cm.
  Includes bibliographical references.
  ISBN 978-0-8066-8052-1 (alk. paper)
  1. Success. 2. Interpersonal relations. 3. Conduct of life. 4. Emotional maturity. I. Title.

BJ1611.2.R515 2008
170'.44--dc22
                                    2008031643

The paper used in this publication meets the minimum requirements of American National Standard for Information Sciences—Permanence of Paper for Printed Library Materials, ANSI Z329.48-1984.

Manufactured in the U.S.A.

12   11   10   09   08   1   2   3   4   5   6   7   8   9   10

❧ CONTENTS ❧

$\mathscr{E}$ ACKNOWLEDGMENTS $\mathscr{F}$

I want to thank the many clients who have allowed me to be a part of their lives as they struggled to work their way through the challenges they faced. I was privileged to learn from them as I watched them use Bowen Family Systems Theory to create new, more satisfying lives for themselves. The clinical stories in this book represent real people, in real situations, and their real outcomes. However, so many facts and details have been changed to protect their identities that even their friends would not recognize them. In some cases clinical stories have been amalgamated.

As will be obvious in the text, I want also to recognize the importance for me of reading Jane Austen's novels. Her stories are so much more than the conventional romantic love stories that Hollywood tends to make of them. They are truly about her characters struggling to become better people, the best they can be, and how this increases their satisfaction and happiness in life. In addition to her wit, her sense of irony, and her exceptional writing, her focus on how to better live the values we profess was instructive for me, and I hope I have relayed some of that to the reader.

Finally, I want to thank my longtime friend Richard Babin, who gave this manuscript a thorough reading and made corrections and improvements that I appreciate. His insights and understanding helped to make this a clearer and more readable text; however, of course, the remaining faults remain totally my responsibility.

✄ INTRODUCTION ✄

Character and emotional maturity

The topic of relationships is one that will always provide fodder for discussion. Recently my wife and I were having a potluck meal with five other couples. One of the couples said that they had just had their tenth anniversary (this was the second marriage for each partner). Others chimed in to say they had recently had an anniversary as well. Lois and I had just celebrated our fortieth. Then the wife in the first couple said, "Well, you guys, what does it take to make a marriage work for so long?"

Everyone had something of value to say about the topic. "Tolerance" and "acceptance" were words that were used quite a bit. I was quite interested in the diversity of views and the different ways people approached the topic. I reflected on all of the couples I had worked with over the years in my clinical practice of marriage and family therapy. I reflected as well on our own experience and said that, in a very general way, there are basically two kinds of couples: those who have strong enough character and enough emotional maturity to work at the inevitable difficulties of marriage and those who don't.

I don't mean to say that these are two distinct groups. No one is black or white on the issues of character and maturity. We all exist on an emotional maturity continuum, and our location on it varies from one area of life to another. No one has it all together.

> Being in love and being loving are two different things. The first is a passive experience that happens to us and can, just as easily, stop happening. The second is an intentional act. It is something we decide to do.

I certainly don't. I don't think of myself as all that mature, and Lois and I have had plenty of difficulty as a result. It has not been an easy forty years of marriage, especially since we are both only children who can still want things to go our way.

Some people think that all it takes for a successful relationship is being in love. Falling in love is a universal human experience that seems to be a part of our human nature. The experience stirs up in us powerful feelings of attraction, sexual heat, and mutual enjoyment that are simply wonderful to experience. Researchers are able to track part of what happens to us emotionally and chemically in our bodies when we fall in love. There really is such a thing as "Love Potion Number 9." It exists in our hormones and it makes us behave in the crazy, obsessive ways we often do when in love.

However, researchers and our own personal experience tell us that the unique experience of being in love wears off. The chemicals involved seem to burn out in anywhere from six months to two years. The magic stops. Life returns to the emotional level it was at before the experience of falling in love. And whatever people have going on in their lives together at that point may not seem like enough. Many couples have taken this as a sign that they ought not to be together.

Being in love and being loving are two different things. The first is a passive experience that happens to us and can, just as easily, stop happening. The second is an intentional act. It is something we decide to do. And again, our ability to do it consistently depends on our level of emotional maturity. With enough maturity we can become people of character, loving people who have good relationships.

The plan of this book

My intent in this book is to define what I mean by character and emotional maturity. I will argue that it takes emotional maturity to be able to consistently live out the qualities of goodness involved in strong character. Primarily, I will focus on emotional maturity, show what I mean by it, and describe how to develop it in our own lives. I will explain the concept and give many examples of people who have worked at becoming more mature. Of course, emotional maturity is not the only factor involved in making relationships work, but it is a big one, a critical one. Emotional maturity gives us the ability to build solid character, to be a person of principle, or to be a good person.

To become people of stronger character, we must be able to address questions such as "How do I want to live my life?" and "What kind of a person do I want to be?" Our ability to arrive at satisfactory answers to these questions will make all the difference in our level of satisfaction and happiness with our lives, whether we are in a relationship or not. I will look at some of the primary reasons we fail to be good people with good relationships. Personal anxiety is at the core of much of this failure.

Then, turning from the analysis of to the development of emotional maturity, I will start with the ability to know one's self as the essential beginning place. This appears to be an easy task, but our own subjectivity often gets in the way and skews our picture of our self. Others see a different picture of who we are, just as we see others differently than they see themselves.

The next ingredient in emotional maturity is being able to take responsibility for who we are and who we might become. We are very clever at finding ways to blame others for our own faults and foibles, and at finding reasons for not changing.

Taking responsibility for self is the first step in creating change in self. Thinking about and setting goals for our growth is how we begin to fulfill the desire to grow and become better people. This means we have to avoid getting sidetracked by some of our feelings. We have to be able to think as clearly and objectively as possible about our lives in relationships in order to know where we are and where to head. Finally, we have to establish the principles by which we will live our lives in relationships so that we can answer questions such as "How do I want to live my life?"

> This is not a book on psychotherapy. Although a specific way of thinking about relationships and emotional maturity does inform it, one does not have to "get into therapy" to understand and use my approach to relationships and emotional maturity.

The approach of this book: Bowen Family Systems Theory and Jane Austen

This is not a book on psychotherapy. Although a specific way of thinking about relationships and emotional maturity does inform it, one does not have to "get into therapy" to understand and use my approach to relationships and emotional maturity, although the clinical setting is where many of my examples will come from. My approach is as old as human beings and is based on something we have been practicing, at one level or another, ever since the human family first formed. It was not invented by therapists.

I use an approach to psychotherapy known as Bowen Family Systems Theory, which assumes that there is a deep interconnection between the biological, psychological, and sociological processes in our lives, and that these are based, first of all, in the family we are born into. This means that no one is simply an isolated individual. Our personal characteristics are influenced by those we have been close to over the years, as well as by our genetic inheritance. We are closely connected emotionally to those we grow up with in our family. We inevitably influence one another significantly. When we go out into the world as young adults, our character has already been deeply influenced by our years of experience with these people. This original emotional system contributes to our level of emotional maturity.

The family is like a mobile where each person is part of a delicately balanced system. When one person moves toward or away from the center of gravity, everyone else is affected and has to adjust. For example, a father who is a successful and wealthy accountant, a partner in his firm, decides to give up his career, buy a motorcycle, and tour the country for a year on his own, chucking everything he has worked for. His wife, his teenage children, his extended network of family and friends, and those he works with are upset with this move on his part. They react emotionally to his decision. The overall balance of the family and workplace is affected and others have to either adjust or try to get him to move back into the responsible position he previously held and to "stop upsetting things with your crazy behavior."

In addition, all kinds of more normal life experiences and unanticipated events, good and bad, affect the family emotional balance. They are like a wind blowing through the mobile. The birth of a baby, the marriage of a grown child, an affair, a divorce, a job promotion or demotion, a move to a different region of the country or just a new neighborhood, recognition for civic achievement, incarceration for criminal behavior, retirement, major illness, disability, and death—these are just a few things that can disturb the emotional system of a family. How emotionally upsetting they are depends on how anxious people become, or how emotionally reactive they are.

These are just simple examples of how we all affect each other in this family mobile. In actual fact, the patterns of influence are much deeper, much more profound, and often much less visible or openly dramatic. The ongoing, repetitive emotional patterns and ways of relating that are unique to each family powerfully shape who we are.

The character and level of emotional maturity of our family of origin will affect how well we can manage the inevitable unbalancing that life brings to our own adult family life. The stronger the character and the more mature the family and its members, the better we will be able to manage the anxiety of unbalancing experiences. We will have greater flexibility and skill in achieving the required rebalancing. The more mature the family, the more it will produce adult people of character who will have the competence to deal with the emotional tasks of life they will face.

In this book, I will focus on the "differentiation of self," just one of the eight basic concepts in Bowen Family Systems Theory. Readers who want to learn more about it can read my book *Family Ties That Bind* for a simple introduction, or they can go to more advanced books listed in the bibliography.

In addition to drawing on Bowen theory and giving illustrations from my own clinical practice, I will use illustrations from the novels of Jane Austen. She is one of my heroes. Not only does she write wonderfully and entertain us with her humor and insight, but her protagonists exemplify what I am talking about in this book. They do not come by their own character and emotional maturity easily. Her books are about their struggles to be good people, to live up to their standards, and how they go about doing it. For example, in *Pride and Prejudice*, Austen shows us exactly what Darcy and Elizabeth have to do to overcome their own pride and prejudices and their emotional reactivity to each other so that they can eventually become a happy couple. Austen demonstrates that the truths of family systems theory were known long before the theory itself was developed.

Who should read this book

This book is for those who want to improve the quality of their lives and character by increasing their level of emotional maturity. As they do so, their close relationships will also improve. The book is a prelude to what makes for good relationships. The concepts and principles discussed here apply to all relationships (such as with friends or colleagues at work), not just our love relationships.

If you are a young adult reading this book, I congratulate you. Surely you are more thoughtful than most people your age and you will find the lessons here valuable as you develop new relationships. People in long-established relationships will also find this book of value in thinking about the normal and ongoing issues they face, and what makes for bettering those relationships.

It is possible that you have already been married and divorced. Perhaps more than once. Like most of us you are trying to find your way through this swamp called relationships and figure out what it is all about, or even overcome the cynicism that can result from previous relationship experiences. As a divorced person, you now comprise a major part of our society. If you are just starting to look for a partner again and feeling somewhat gun-shy, you will find help here in thinking through some of the difficult and confusing thoughts and feelings you have. And I can guarantee that it will make the experience a much more interesting and less painful one.

A personal statement

My biggest fear in writing this book is that it might sound moralistic. Moralism is a way of dealing with our own felt inadequacies by projecting them onto others and judging them as inadequate. That is not my intent. We all have problems in living caused primarily by our emotional immaturity. We all do things that could have been done in a much better way, with less negative repercussions. We all have room for growth. That is as true of me as it is of anyone.

My hope is that the reader will be able to maintain a sense of compassion, first for self and then for others. I believe that we are all doing as well as we can at the moment. In my best moments, I can have that attitude toward myself and with those I am close to. I think I always had it in my work as a therapist. The acceptance of self as we are is, paradoxically, essential to personal change.

It is still quite easy for me to slip back into the old feelings of that lonely little boy I was growing up, detached from others, living in my own private world. I believed no one was interested in me. I made my peace with that and adapted accordingly. I can feel compassion for myself as a child. The specific patterns of life and ways of relating I created around that experience made sense in that context. But they have never fit my life as an adult. That is a problem we all face. We construct our lives while growing up within one emotional context, but as adults we are living in a different world where those old ways of being usually don't fit. Most of us continue to live "as if" we are still back in that old context.

While this book is not meant as a list of moral values and virtues that people should emulate, you will in fact find some of my values explicitly and implicitly stated here. I don't know how to get around this. I cannot act as if I don't have them. They come out of a generally Christian set of beliefs. So to some extent, I will inevitably be listing some of my ethical beliefs, primarily in the examples I use. But they are not the point of this effort. You the reader most likely have your own set of ethical beliefs and commitments. What we are both up against is how to fulfill in our daily lives the things we say we are committed to.

I am lucky to have had people in my life who accepted my ways and who were forgiving and compassionate around my errors. I am deeply thankful for that. To move ahead in life, however, I could not simply count on the compassion and understanding of others. To keep desired relationships and to achieve what I wanted in life, I had to change; I had to become better, and I have, although I am definitely not yet at my "best." We are all still works in progress.

This book is about what I have learned and continue to learn in striving to become a better person. I hope you find it useful in your own life journey.

EMOTIONAL MATURITY:
A KEY TO GOOD RELATIONSHIPS

Where is the problem in our relationships?

We have all heard the statistics. More than 50 percent of marriages end in divorce. An even higher percentage of second marriages fail, and it is higher yet for third marriages. There is debate about the accuracy of these statistics and whether the divorce rate is really as high as this. But whatever is true, we know that marriages are in difficulty. We all know people who have been divorced, and probably remarried. This might even be true of you.

There is a reason that second marriages have been called "the triumph of hope over experience." Ever hopeful about marriage and desirous of what it can offer, many of us don't seem to learn from one marriage to the next about how to overcome its built-in challenges. As a marriage and family therapist for more than thirty years, I have been intimately involved in helping people wrestle with these challenges.

The research is clear about the damage to everyone involved when there is a divorce. No one gets out of a marriage unscathed. Each partner suffers emotionally, in varying degrees, and there is now some good evidence that even physical health is affected by a divorce. Clearly, in most cases, the children suffer; if not from the divorce then from the upsetting conditions that led to the divorce and often continue between the parents after the divorce is final. Divorce causes disruption in the larger extended family as well, and as the numbers of divorces accumulate, there is significant fallout in society as well.

I am not against divorce. I am glad people can get out of relationships when they find they can no longer exist within them. But clearly something needs to change in the way we go about choosing our partners, the way we get to know each other, and the way we manage ourselves in our ongoing relationships with one another. As a therapist, I have observed that too many people are divorcing unnecessarily. I have come to believe that a higher percentage of people could create more satisfying relationships in marriage.

Partly we are misdiagnosing the problem; we are placing responsibility for the problems in the wrong place. We tend to speak of "relationships" as if they were things in themselves. When they first come to see me, clients often say, "Our relationship is in trouble." They want "the relationship" fixed. They complain, "The relationship has become unworkable," and say that they have "worked at trying to improve the relationship." Ultimately, if they divorce, they say that "the relationship has failed."

This diagnosis ignores the fact that it is two people who make a relationship what it is. A relationship is not a thing. It has no responsibility of its own or ability to exist on its own. It is simply a process that results from the way two people interact with one another. It is no better or worse than they are. Rarely do I get a client coming in saying, "I don't like the way I am behaving in my marriage and I want to change. I want to be a better person in my relationships."

> Rarely do I get a client coming in saying, "I don't like the way I am behaving in my marriage and I want to change. I want to be a better person in my relationships."

Few of us like to own up to it, but our own personal emotional immaturity is a major part of the difficulty in our relationships; this usually goes back to relationship issues with our families of origin and the way we continue to manage our lives with those people today. What is unresolved with our families is likely, in some form, to be unresolved with our adult partners.

Character and relationships

The argument of this book is that character is the essential ingredient in good relationships. People of good character tend to be happier people in the sense that they are more satisfied with their lives. People who have strong, mature characters, tested in the crucible of difficult circumstances and challenging issues over time, are going to make better relationships. Relationships that last and are satisfying and happy will inevitably be lived by people of good character—the essential ingredient of good relationships. They can call on it in the difficult times and in the emotional intensity of close relationships.

I mean "character" in a very broad sense, not in any narrow sense that some of us may have grown up with in church (for example, "People of good character don't drink, swear, smoke, or go out with people who do.") Character is not just about our personal ethics; it is about our approach to all of life and all our relationships, and the kind of emotional maturity we bring to these. There are many choices to be made as we live our lives, some of them very difficult. The choices we make, for good or ill, at particular crossroads will depend primarily on our character. As is commonly said, "Character is destiny."

My *Webster's Collegiate Dictionary* gives eight meanings for the word *character*. One meaning is "the attributes and features that make up and distinguish the individual," but this could be any sort of distinctive personality trait or characteristic. In using the word *character*, I am referring to another meaning: "moral excellence and firmness."

Some of us can get a little twitchy and uneasy around that word *moral*. We often hesitate to use the word. It does not always sound like high praise to say that someone is very moral. The word has come to have connotations of rigid uprightness in a kind of prickly way that makes others feel uncomfortable. Instead, we may say that a person is good. Generally, by this we mean that he or she lives by certain moral principles such as kindness, caring, respect and concern for others, honesty and truthfulness, and faithfulness. These are a few qualities of goodness that contribute to a person having a strong character.

Character is about our moral strength. It is not some trait we are born with or that we simply have or don't have. Just as with physical strength, to develop moral strength requires hard work and exercise. It is a matter of choice. And our choices decide for us the kind of life we will have—and whether we will be satisfied with that life. Looks, athleticism, wealth, intelligence, career, and where we live are the things people tend to focus on as ways to achieve a happy life. But we can have all of these to the hilt and, if character is lacking, we will not be happy. We may have plenty of pleasurable moments, but overall they will not satisfy. Character is something we all have to work at and develop throughout our lives. No one is born with character.

To what extent do we think about *our own* character? About what *we* bring to a relationship morally? How *we* contribute to the relationship's "goodness"? The failure to do so seems to be part of human nature. We are much more likely to focus on our partner and his or her failures and problems than we are to reflect on our own. We tend to be other-focused rather than self-focused when it comes to issues of character. We are often experts at critiquing others and ignorant about our own foibles. How often do we ask, "In what ways am I difficult to live with? How do I contribute to the problems of this relationship? How am I failing to live up to the standards I apply to others?"

Popular culture, as represented in the media, does not offer us much of substance to help with these challenges. Is this the media's fault? I don't know. There is some reason to agree with them when they say they only show what people want to see. Many of us do seem to enjoy watching people behaving badly—as they often do in "reality TV." Even the fiction we read tends to be about how people screw up their lives and make them worse rather than how they make them better. All of this can contribute to the kind of cynicism we have today about relationships. We may think, "No one has good relationships today; they are not possible. Why bother trying?"

However, we know that this is not totally true. While nearly all of us can improve, many of us are good enough people in good enough relationships. Hopefully, we also know people with truly good relationships who have something to show us about how they live their lives. This is the best antidote to cynicism. If we personally know people who have demonstrated strong character in how they live their lives and meet the challenges of life and relationships, then we ourselves can be more hopeful and perhaps even learn from them. Ideally, we grew up with parents like this. But it seems like fewer and fewer people today, growing up in their families, have seen good relationships at work. And as a consequence, they have developed fewer personal resources for making their own good relationships and for being better people in those relationships.

> How often do we ask, "In what ways am I difficult to live with? How do I contribute to the problems of this relationship? How am I failing to live up to the standards I apply to others?"

Emotional maturity versus emotional reactivity

Being a good person of solid character involves having the courage to live according to the self-chosen principles that character is based on. This is essential to living a happy, satisfying life and having good relationships. We arrive at our level of goodness or character through the development of our emotional maturity.

Emotional maturity gives us the strength to become the person we want to be, to become our best. Our close relationships can quickly reveal our level of emotional maturity. Most of us are highly attuned to what others think of us. Our feelings may go up and down with this variable. We are happy when they appear to think well of us and unhappy when they are critical of us. I call this reactivity. The reactive feelings we experience in our relationships are most often in charge of our behavior. If someone close to us seems to regularly disapprove of us, we react to this. We may become depressed and feel hopeless, or we may become angry and go on the counterattack, or we may become sullen and withdraw, or maybe, if we feel deeply hurt, we may even cut off from them entirely.

The point is that our feelings, rather than our principles for living, often guide our behavior. Let's say I want to embody in my life the principles of considerateness and kindness. But if my partner criticizes me and puts me down, I may lose the ability to stay focused on those principles. Then I will be more focused on my critical partner and react to her in some probably inconsiderate and unkind way. I will want to get back at her or, at a minimum, pull away from her.

A principle-focused life is one in which we want to live our lives generally, and specifically with others who are important to us, on the basis of our principles regardless of how others are with us. A feeling-focused life is one in which we are always reacting to others, sometimes positively and sometimes negatively. How we are is affected by how they are with us. We forget our principles. In a real sense, in a feeling-focused life others are in charge of our lives. And if they react to our negative reaction to them, then we are in charge of them emotionally. Then it is off to the races; the fight is on, revealing less emotional maturity and more emotional reactivity on both our parts.

I have seen clients who have wrestled with emotional difficulties like a highly reactive, angry nature. Those who have achieved their goal of getting these difficulties under control have demonstrated a fair amount of growth in character. They became morally better people. They achieved this strengthening of character primarily by working at their level of emotional maturity and becoming less reactive to others.

In a sense, they grew themselves up. They became more mature. They identified certain principles they wanted to live by, like being less judgmental and more tolerant, more kind and considerate, or perhaps learned to feel braver when feeling alone and anxious. This was very hard work for them. They paid less attention to the old, reactive feelings that had previously run their lives and began to live by certain standards or principles that they had decided were important to maintain. Doing this made their lives better, they felt better about themselves, and their relationships improved as well.

Nearly all of us profess to believe in certain values and say we have some standards of goodness. However, our ability to live up to our own professed standards is a different matter. I often fail to live up to mine, usually because of my emotional reactivity. Emotional maturity is the critical factor in the ability to live a life consistent with what we profess to believe in. The degree to which we have achieved a certain amount of this maturity determines the degree of our success in many areas of life, not just the marital relationship.

Becoming a better person, a person of principle, inevitably requires courage. There are critical turning points in our lives where standing by our principles will feel risky. It might even cost us in some real way. People who stand by their principles have been known to lose their jobs, their marital partners, their family, their inheritance, and their friends. But these people, as they weigh the losses against losing respect for themselves and what they stand for, make the choice for principle. It is not an easy thing to do.

> Becoming a better person, a person of principle, inevitably requires courage. There are critical turning points in our lives where standing by our principles will feel risky.

The most interesting thing, however, is that these are the people who ultimately have the best relationships. The kind of principled, mature people I am talking about do not self-righteously live their principles like they were divine law, and they do not lay down their law to others or judgmentally evaluate others by their standards. They are just clear about how *they* will live their own lives and what *they* will or will not do at any particular juncture. They have the virtue that most of us would call wisdom.

Developing our emotional maturity

Normally we have developed our particular level of emotional maturity by the time we leave home as young adults. It is generally something we "catch" from life in our family. This is not about school knowledge, or attitudes, or even relational skills as such. We can be ignorant about a lot of things and still be relatively mature. Or we can have an IQ of 150 and still be pretty immature emotionally.

So the emotional maturity of our family has a lot to do with our own emotional maturity, or at least where we start in adult life. The higher the degree of our parents' maturity, the higher our own is likely to be. The higher the level of emotional reactivity in our family, the more likely we are also to be less mature. As adults, we find that growing our level of emotional maturity is challenging work. It isn't easy. Only by dint of significant intentional effort can we take that level of maturity beyond what we developed within our families.

This book is not just about the specific characteristics of good people; it is about what it takes personally to consistently live out the values of good character. It goes beyond the techniques, skills, and procedures that make up many relationship books. As a therapist, I know most of the techniques one can use to make relationships work better, but personally, in the heat of an argument with my wife, I can totally lose touch with those skills. What we need in such moments is something more basic and deeper than techniques. We need the personal strengths required to practice them in times of tension and uneasiness.

There is a paucity of examples of people with good character making good relationships. We have few models. I'm sure they exist, but we don't hear much about them. We know of such people in history. Certain names come to mind automatically—people who lived and died for their principles: certainly Jesus would be one; Thomas More, who stood up for what he believed against Henry VIII, who declared himself the head of the English church; Gandhi, who confronted the British and eventually won freedom for India; Abraham Lincoln, who saw what was right with regard to slavery and abolished it; Martin Luther King Jr., who gave his life, along with many others, for the cause of greater civil rights; and Rosa Parks, who decided she would sit where she wanted to on a public bus. The list could go on and on. These people made our world a better place to live in and showed us how to be better people.

Where are the real heroes of good character and good relationships today? It seems like there are very few, and those who exist get little attention. Who is showing us how to be good and how to make satisfying relationships? Near the top of my list would be Nelson Mandela, who endured years of imprisonment and torture and then became the president of his country, leading it into an incredible spirit of reconciliation. He demonstrated great emotional maturity when he did not reactively become focused on revenge.

Sometimes we can find examples of heroes in our own family. My Aunt Blanche and Uncle Alton lived in St. Louis all of their adult lives, much of that time in an old brick house on Waterman Street. When they moved there, the neighborhood consisted of all white people. Over the years, as the racial makeup of the area began to change, the white people began moving out. My aunt and uncle decided to stay. They said there was no reason they couldn't be neighborly with these new people. Eventually they were the only white people left in an all-black neighborhood—and they made many new, good friends. They were active in their community and worked with others to improve the quality of life there for everyone. When they each died, their new neighbors were there and were a major help to me when I had to close up my aunt and uncle's house and deal with their affairs. They knew my aunt and uncle to be good people.

> Psychotherapy is just starting to pay attention to the importance of values with regard to people's life, health, and well-being.

This is what I mean by character. They had a goodness that was not influenced by the strong racial prejudices of their day. And they had the emotional maturity to stand by their principles and fulfill their commitments. Of course, my aunt and uncle also had their own personal foibles and problems in life like the rest of us. When the chips were down, however, they made a choice for goodness that many of their former white neighbors could not manage.

Character and happiness

The field of relationship therapy, instead of focusing on good character, has tended to emphasize techniques and relational skills like listening and communication, expression of feelings, fair fights, problem solving and negotiation, techniques for having a better sexual relationship, and so forth. Of course, these are important skills, but what is often forgotten is the kind of emotional maturity required to achieve and consistently practice these sorts of skills in the sometimes heated atmosphere of our relationships.

Psychotherapy is just starting to pay attention to the importance of values with regard to people's life, health, and well-being. For example, Dr. Martin Seligman, the former president of the American Psychological Association, has recently written a highly praised book called *Authentic Happiness*. Along with several other important qualities, he points out the important role that strong character and personal virtue play in our happiness and emotional health. He decries the loss of focus on the development of good character in our society. He identifies six virtues that tend to be pervasive in nearly all cultures and religions: (1) wisdom and knowledge; (2) courage; (3) love and humanity; (4) justice; (5) temperance; and (6) spirituality and transcendence. These are important virtues to engender for our own health and well-being. Doing so will also bring us happiness and satisfaction in life.

Jane Austen and our relationships

Jane Austen's books often illustrate what I mean by emotional maturity and strength of character. She wrote of these things long before psychotherapy was discovered or thought of. I see a strong similarity between her character-based understanding of how good relationships work and my own therapeutic ideas about better functioning in relationships. It is popular to think of Jane Austen's novels as simply romantic courtship stories combined with a comedy of manners. Hollywood has tended to do this to her books. Jane Austen is, however, much more important and relevant to our topic than that. She has done serious, critical thinking about relationships, and she is specifically focused on our topic of how to be a better person in our relationships. In the condensed form that novels offer, and in a more entertaining way than offered by my clinical reports, she shows how it is done and what it takes.

In her day, novels were criticized (mostly by men) as not being "serious" literary works. Nonfiction was thought to be the only important, serious kind of writing that people could learn from. However, her clergyman father had a large library of fiction as well as nonfiction, and he encouraged all of his children to read and discuss it. One of Austen's early books, *Northanger Abbey*, is a parody of the gothic romance genre that was popular then. Early in that book, Austen presents her well-known defense of the novel as a serious and weighty form of writing. In chapter 5, she writes of two of the main, young female characters shutting themselves up on rainy, wet mornings to read novels. Then she says, addressing the readers of her day:

> Yes, novels . . .
> —there seems almost a general wish of decrying the capacity and undervaluing the labour of the novelist, and of slighting the performances which have only genius, wit, and taste to recommend them.
> —"I am no novel-reader
> —I seldom look into novels
> —Do not imagine that I often read novels
> —It is really very well for a novel."
> Such is the common cant.
> —"And what are you reading, Miss—?"
> "Oh! It is only a novel!" replies the young lady, while she lays down her book with affected indifference, or momentary shame.
> —"It is only Cecilia, or Camilla, or Belinda";
> or, in short, only some work in which the greatest powers of the mind are displayed, in which the most thorough knowledge of human nature, the happiest delineation of its varieties, the liveliest effusions of wit and humour, are conveyed to the world in the best-chosen language.

In spite of significant social and cultural differences between her world and ours, human nature has not changed. Jane Austen understands us. She sees our personal strengths and foibles and knows the elements that go into building character, emotionally and intellectually. Even with obvious differences in language and cultural mores between her times and ours, it is easy to believe that she is writing about us.

Austen found examples of greatness and moral courage in ordinary people and the decisions of everyday life. She shows us, in realistic terms, how a poor and otherwise inconsequential figure like Fanny Price can become the emotional center and moral leader of a prominent, wealthy family like the Bertrams of *Mansfield Park*. And she accomplishes this with "genius, wit, and taste," thoroughly entertaining us in the process.

Austen challenges us to think about ourselves and how we manage our part in relationships. She is really writing about what it takes to be an emotionally mature human being within the emotionally challenging context of human community. Courtship and the powerful dramas of falling in love are the exciting, fun, and age-appropriate experiences her young protagonists engaged in on their way to becoming strong, principled, and important members of society. For Austen, being a better person leads to better and happier relationships.

I am looking at Austen through the lens of how she can help us today with our relationships. What many of us appreciate in her novels is the internal, character-based strength of her heroes and the nature of their relationships with others. If we focus just on how people actually behave in relationships, rather than on culture and language, there is in fact a lot of similarity between her world and ours. After all, we share the same human nature.

❦ Two ❧

GOOD PEOPLE
MAKE GOOD RELATIONSHIPS

Principle and character in relationships

What makes for good relationships? Ask this question to a group of people in my profession of marriage and family therapy and you may hear about communication skills and techniques like active listening, eye contact, expression of feelings, use of "I" statements rather than "you" statements, problem solving, conflict resolution, and assertiveness. The list could go on. Each of these is useful and does improve the quality of relationships.

I am, however, suggesting that "good people make good relationships." This is most likely the answer that Jane Austen would give to the question of what makes for good relationships. The focus here is not on communication techniques, or relationship techniques, or even techniques for expressing feelings, but on the maturity of the character of the person who uses them. End of story? End of book? No. Obviously the answer is not that simple.

The character of individuals and families is what makes up the character of our culture, our society, and our national identity. Character is revealed in many small actions in our lives, and most of us have some. We leave a tip for a waiter in a restaurant that we know we will never visit again. It is not in our self-interest to do this, but it is good. Most of us pay our taxes out of a belief that we should, not just out of fear of prosecution since clearly that so often does not happen. We find a wallet on the street and we try to find who it belongs to because we all know what it would be like to lose a wallet. We don't litter deserted beaches even though no one would see us do it and a

> Good people, people of character, will base their behavior, in life generally as well as in their relationships, on certain self-chosen principles for living.

candy wrapper in such a large expanse is no big deal. The list of things we do just because it is right is endless. We don't all do all of them. Each of us neglects certain areas of correct behavior, but by and large we are supportive of social goodness.

There is now a growing body of research evidence showing that people who have good marriages, or people who are simply considered healthy psychologically, also are good people. There are researchers looking at moral attitudes such as gratitude, altruism, forgiveness, and compassion. These attitudes represent principles for living. They are values that were once emphasized in the training of children, and adults were expected to emulate them. In our modern world, principles like these are often forgotten.

Good people, people of character, will base their behavior, in life generally as well as in their relationships, on certain self-chosen principles for living. For example, a man decides he will not gossip about his coworkers. If someone in his office wants to talk to him about a third person who is not present, the man will not participate and will make it clear in his behavior that he does not do this. He does not tell others that it is wrong to gossip; he just doesn't do it. He may ask the gossiper a related question about himself every time the gossiper mentions someone else. Or a woman may decide she will not "suck up" to her boss, but will let him know clearly and directly what she thinks are the difficulties about a specific plan he has proposed rather than talking to her coworkers about his "awful" plan.

Our self-chosen principles are usually arrived at over time and are more or less consciously held. They are mostly derived from and tested in the crucible of experience. These principles are the foundational basis that provides guidance for how more mature people will conduct themselves. They define how they will and won't behave at specific important junctions of decision making, particularly in the kind of difficult and emotionally challenging circumstances that can occur in relationships. Their principles are an integral part of their self, of their sense of personal identity. To act out of these principles in difficult circumstances, rather than simply to react to the immature behavior of others, is a way to be true to self. There is a kind of consistent goodness to them.

What is goodness?

My dictionary gives more than twenty ways of using the word *good*. Originally, the old English word *good* had a connection with the concept of "God." What was good derived from God. When we say "good-bye," that is a short way of saying, "God be with you." The biblical creation story tells us that, looking at the creation, God said it was "good." The word *good* has a strong moral connotation, but it also can include the qualities of bountifulness, fertility, beauty, suitableness, wholeness as well as wholesomeness, benevolence, competence, skill, and praiseworthiness. Because it was something that came from God, the word *good* was primarily used to denote virtue.

We often use the word *good* in other ways today. If our dinner host asks us if we would like another serving of food, we might say, "No thanks, I'm good," as in *satisfied*. If a parent asks a teen if he wants to take a coat when he goes out, the teen may rebuff the parent, saying, "No, I'm good." Less and less today does "good" mean something about one's virtue, and more and more it refers to a state of satisfaction. Also, in youth culture, "I'm bad" has come to mean "I'm really good" at whatever endeavor is being attempted. The same is true of "wicked." The irony in these statements affirms, in its way, the importance of goodness.

By *good* I do not mean some moralistic, rigid obedience to certain laws, nor do I mean self-righteously following a prescribed set of rules. All faith positions, liberal or conservative, can be made into a rigid, rules-for-righteousness approach, or they can be lived in a more adaptive and flexible way that requires thoughtfulness, consideration, and an essentially humble, benevolent, and compassionate stance toward others. Wanting to be "generous and respectful" are principles some people seek to live by. How they are expressed in specific circumstances and relationships has to be thought through as a part of each unique experience. Having rules for these experiences would not be adequate for achieving the good.

The definition of what is good will vary depending on a person's cultural context and faith commitments. I have a Christian bias in my use of the word. This will be clear in most of the examples I give, but I believe people of any faith background, or no specific faith background, can still make use of the word for developing their own good relationships.

Some of the classical virtues, which we find in Jane Austen's writing, are prudence (what today we call wisdom), fortitude (bravery or courage in the face of adversity), justice, and temperance (not being run by or overcome by our feelings, being able to control our "temper"). Her heroes also demonstrate, in varying degrees, the Christian virtues of faith, hope, and love. All of these are values I personally would affirm and want to uphold in my life. Whether I am able to do that depends on my level of emotional maturity.

Goodness and character in starting relationships

It used to be that courtship was primarily about getting to know each other's character. While we don't speak much of courtship today, the process is still the same. The issue is not simply about getting a partner, but finding a good one. And that, of course, depends on one's values for what is good. Today people may still be interested in finding good partners, but how they define *good* and the values they use to choose a partner may be quite different, and perhaps inadequate. People commit themselves to one another without knowing much about who the other person is, or really knowing the person's character. We make assumptions about who the other is. The apparent "good catch" may not actually be so good. In starting a relationship, we want to discover this before a firm commitment is made.

To find a partner of good character, we first have to look at ourselves. Too many people focus just on the other person. If we have not looked adequately at the maturity of our own character and the values implicit in that character, then we will necessarily choose poorly. The relationship will not, most likely, go as well as we had wished. Who we are makes a great difference in the kind of person we choose. The issue is not just about the character of the other person.

> Who we are makes a great difference in the kind of person we choose. The issue is not just about the character of the other person.

In getting started working with couples in therapy, I routinely took a history of their relationship, starting with courtship. Very often, the behavior they were complaining about in their partner, "x" years down the road of marriage, was there at the very beginning of their relationship—but they didn't notice it. I would say something like, "Isn't it interesting that he/she was doing 'that' at the very beginning of your relationship. What do you think was going on with you that you didn't notice?" Of course, they usually don't know, but the question implicates them in the difficulties by suggesting there was something about them as choosers also involved. It is not just about the other person.

Fiction often contains much relational truth. Jane Austen's books are about people striving to become better people as they face the difficult emotional challenges of life and relationships. Choosing a life partner is one of the challenges. Her stories are about young women (and men) defining themselves within their families and in their society in order to become more mature adults, ready to take on the challenges of life, including the challenge of choosing their partners in life. Her characters know that the ability to choose a partner wisely has to do with their own values and how they influence their choices. This issue is at the core of a book like *Pride and Prejudice*. It is when Elizabeth Bennet recognizes that she has not known herself well enough that she can then begin to see the merits of Darcy. The fact that she had preferred Wickham over Darcy was a critical mistake for her as "chooser."

Willoughby, in *Sense and Sensibility*, is a prime example of a young man who has everything going for him and who might have achieved a life of love and happiness if he had been able to be faithful to Marianne—but

In Jane Austen's Sense and Sensibility, Marianne sees the world of men divided into exciting studs and boring duds. This romantic fantasy creates some serious blind spots for her: she sees neither his flaws and faults nor her own. She is also blind to her true needs in a relationship. In effect, she knows neither herself nor Willoughby well enough to choose him as someone to be intimately related with.

- Reflect on what your blind spots might be when choosing someone to be in a close relationship with.

- Consider talking with someone who knows you well (and whom you trust) about how he or she sees your blind spots.

THERE ARE NONE SO BLIND
AS THOSE WHO WILL NOT SEE!

his character is deeply flawed. "Each faulty propensity" in him, Austen says, is bound to lead him into a poor relationship and a less-than-happy life. Marianne Dashwood, as a chooser, also brings a flawed character to the relationship, and that is part of what leads her into an unworkable relationship with Willoughby, and even puts her life at risk.

Marianne sees the world of men as divided into (in our words) exciting studs and boring duds. She is attracted to the charming, lively, handsome, socially talented stud who is Willoughby. Her romantic fantasy and the values that go with it blind her to his faults. Because of these personal faults, she misses clues about him that are right in front of her. Her romantic fantasy leads her to believe she intuitively knows who he is without asking many specific questions. The result, of course, is that she does not truly know him. The same set of romantic values leads her to reject both Colonel Brandon and her sister Elinor's love, Edward Ferrars, as "duds." They don't measure up to her more superficial, romantic vision of what a man should be. Anyone who has ever experienced an infatuation can identify with Marianne.

We understand her attraction to Willoughby. In many ways, he fits our own contemporary ideas of what a "good catch" would be. He brings excitement, warmth, wit, status, and a kind of dashing zest for life that is highly attractive. And he is good looking, has a sparkling personality, and is mostly well mannered. It feels good to Marianne to attract his attentions. To her mind, it says something positive about her that she is able to hook (a term she would say she "hates") a man like him. She feels good about herself with Willoughby beside her. The proof of this is what happens to her when he abandons her. Her life is not worth living if he is not with her.

Willoughby, however, is deeply dishonest with her and simply gives her a line in order to win her affection. He seeks "his own guilty triumph" at her expense. As he confesses to Elinor at the end of the novel, he had had no intention of returning her affection. He ends up being the real "dud." He says in chapter 44:

> "When I first became intimate in your family, I had no other intention, no other view in the acquaintance, than to pass my time pleasantly while I was obliged to remain in Devonshire. . . . Your sister's lovely person, and interesting manners, could not but please me. . . . But at first, I must confess, my vanity only was elevated by

it. Careless of her happiness, thinking only of my own amusement, giving way to feelings which I had always been too much in the habit of indulging, I endeavoured, by every means in my power, to make myself pleasing to her, without any design of returning her affection."

Haven't we known people like this? This is the guy who is willing to do whatever it takes to get a woman into bed. He has no serious intent. He gives out a line. He portrays himself as someone other than who he is. Willoughby was surprised to find that he actually fell in love with Marianne while pursuing her, but she was not what he was looking for in a wife. His standards for the woman he would ultimately marry were rather shallow. She only had to be a good-enough-looking woman with enough money to support his lifestyle.

Unlike Willoughby, most people are not intentionally dishonest with each other during courtship. But a fair amount of personal vanity, as he says, can be involved in our relationships. We often put great store in how others see us, and we want to look good in the eyes of our partner. In a sense, like Willoughby, we make ourselves pleasing to others to win them over without thinking much about what is truly important to us in life.

Austen gives us clues as to the kind of people Willoughby and Marianne are, and how their choosing of one another, and their behavior, is going to lead to a relational shipwreck. But it takes emotional maturity to see the clues, and that is where Marianne needs to change and grow. A young man may have everything going for him in terms of good looks, material wealth, and an easy, pleasing manner. But if his character is flawed, he is not a good catch. Many women discover this when it is "too late."

And what he looks for in a partner will reflect his own superficial values. If the young man is looking for the beauty queen who will catch the eyes of all the other guys, then he needs her to be beautiful in order to say to the other guys, "Hey, I must be good to be able to catch a looker like her. You must envy me, right?" He needs the woman as an object, like a possession, in order to enhance his own sense of himself. This is part of what Austen means by "vanity."

Being a self in marriage and family life

There is a *New Yorker* cartoon with a very glum-looking middle-aged couple sitting in an office with a marital therapist. In summing up his assessment of them, the therapist says, "Well, you are both miserable people, but I guess that is beside the point." While no therapist would ever say this, most of us have had this kind of couple in therapy. And the comment is *not* beside the point. We each bring our own particular kind of "miserableness" to our relationships, and this generally comes from our earlier important relationships within our families of origin. We come into our adult relationships with a fair amount of "emotional baggage."

Most of us have no idea how much of our adult life is shaped by our experience growing up in our families and by our continuing relationships with those people. Many of us may think in terms of "what they did to me." But we tend not to think about "how I am with them." We may be unhappy with our family, for a variety of reasons. When we reach the age of maturity, we often think that by physically moving away from family we have left all of "that" behind us, especially if we minimize contact with them. We see young adulthood as a time when we can really be ourselves without their interference. But if we think the difficulties were just about them and don't see our part in the overall emotional process, we will miss a critical part of what makes our present relationships work the way they do. We will also fail to see what we bring to our new relationships as adults.

All close relationships inevitably involve forces and pressures in which one person is trying to change another person into being what he or she wants and feels most comfortable with.

In fact, we usually know very little about how to be a self, how to hang on to our own sense of who we are and what we believe in a close adult relationship, if we don't know how to do that with our own family. It is relatively easy "to be a self" if we are living just on our own and staying emotionally distant from others. However, in marriage we often deal with each other the same way we deal with our families. After all, that is what we know about dealing with others in close relationships. Here is a simple example. Growing up, when I had conflicts with my mother I would shut up and withdraw. Then I behaved the same way with my wife early in my marriage.

All close relationships inevitably involve forces and pressures in which one person is trying to change another person into being what he or she wants and feels most comfortable with. That is normal. It is the rare family that does not work this way, and marriage most often works this way. This is what most marital struggles consist of. Our complaints usually focus on what the other person is, or is not, and how we want the other person to be different. The other person is the same with us, trying to change us to be what he or she wants.

Many of us try to deal with the reality of this pressure from our partner to be the way our partner wants by distancing ourselves physically or emotionally. We probably did this with our families and still do this with anyone else who leans on us to be the way *they* want us to be. Some people move thousands of miles away from family in order to be the people they want to be. This is not a solution that will work, no matter how much they find their families manipulative, embarrassing, and difficult. The distance reduces the pressure, but it doesn't change things. They will often find a partner who they think is not like their family and who will help them escape their family, but this too rarely works. Even if they manage to never have contact with family again, the same kinds of emotional issues will rear up in the marriage. The specific content of the issues will likely be different, but the challenge to our own level of maturity will be the same.

Even though this book focuses on the character of individuals, the individual is not the primary focus in my personal approach. We are all part of larger wholes like the family (what I call an emotional system), and who we are is deeply shaped by that original emotional context. But we are also the source of change if it is going to happen at all in our close relationships. Someone within an emotional system has to work at being different before the system itself can function differently. Those contemplating change have to take into account the powerful emotional forces at work in the larger systems that they are a part of as well as how the system will resist their attempts to change. Making changes in how we relate to emotionally powerful others requires courage, another value essential to good relationships.

Developing and defining a self within emotionally close relationships, while staying close to those we know and love, is the way to become a more emotionally mature human being and to establish good relationships. Emotionally mature people exhibit strong personal qualities of character and individuality in the midst of the powerful emotional forces of family and social life. If they can't do it there, then they are unlikely to be able to do it in their other important relationships.

Jane Austen once wrote to a relative that the topic in her novels is "three or four families in a country village." She did not say her stories were about couples, or about this or that young woman and the man she courts and marries. We tend to think her novels are about Elizabeth and Darcy, or Emma and Mr. Knightley, or the other central characters in her stories, and how they eventually marry. But in fact, she is writing about families, set in the larger emotional context of communities, with all of the emotional forces involved in each of these. And in the midst of these settings, her heroes are attempting to become good, emotionally mature human beings. They seek to improve relationships with those they are close to without giving up self and their own values. They are striving to be better people while staying connected to others.

❧ THREE ❧

IS VIRTUE BORING,
OR BAD?

Virtue, relationships, and happiness

More and more, happiness in our society is associated with material wealth, good looks, good jobs, successful children, popularity and inclusion in the "in" group, and so forth. Many of the TV makeover programs have this idea as their premise. Once the house, or the person, or the relationship has been "made over," then people will be happy, and, as proof, the shows generally end with everyone being ecstatic about the results. But experience and research indicate that the ecstasy will be fleeting. They will still be the same people living within these new houses or clothes or skins—and there lies the real problem.

Lasting happiness does not come from these more superficial things. When we read the phrase "the pursuit of happiness" in the Declaration of Independence, some of us may tend to think it is about getting these "things." But it is really about having the *freedom* to become good people and to live a life of goodness, as each person defines it, without having some outside authority tell us what we must do. The framers of the Declaration had the same philosophical basis for happiness as did Aristotle, who said, "The happy people are the good people."

> Character is built by attempting to live a life of virtue in the midst of all of the challenges of life.

We are all interested in being happy, but happiness is a by-product of developing our character. Character is built by attempting to live a life of virtue in the midst of all of the challenges of life. Those who do not make the difficult choices for virtue end up living a less-than-happy life. I saw this in my clinical practice all the time. Happiness does not depend on having wealth and an easier life. Many less-than-admirable characters have wealth and ease, and quite often, they are not happy; their lives don't work. My clinical practice in one of the wealthiest parts of Canada was full of rich people, and I can say categorically that money did not make them happy. Of course, there is no romance to being poor either; having money is better than not having it. The primary issue, however, is virtue or goodness—not money.

Jane Austen also makes a case for the importance of virtue, reason, and self-control in life and love, and in the service of one's life goals. The overarching goal for her is virtue. *Sense and Sensibility* is practically a didactic primer on how this is done. Reason and self-control are the means for developing a virtuous and thus a happy life. Her heroes are not only interesting and engaging; they can also *think* about what is important. They usually don't make the same mistake twice. Emma is the exception. She is slower to learn, but she does. They all learn through experience how to live better lives and make good decisions in their relationships. They will be happier people whether they get their man or not.

From time to time, most of us display some evidence of weak character in minor or major ways. For example, we have blown up at our partners and attacked them—silently in our own minds if not out loud. Or we have withdrawn and refused to talk about an important issue. We have failed to give compliments and to show appreciation. We have evaded, been defensive with, blamed, and judged our partners. We have found ways to diminish others and elevate ourselves. We have been selfish and unloving.

Or, in other contexts, some of us may pad our expense accounts, read confidential material we have found lying in someone else's office, cheat on how many hours we actually work, fail to report income to the tax people, cheat in writing down our golf score, lie to our partner about where we have been, flirt behind our partner's back, lie for a friend to his or her partner, give a line (lie) to get another person in bed just to have sex, or maybe even have sex with the partner of our best friend. But nearly all of us know that these things are not really good for us, for our relationships, and for society. We would not want other people behaving this way with us.

All of us have good and bad in us. We all have moral challenges and shortcomings. It is not really helpful to self-righteously divide the world into bad people and good people, black and white. We are all varying shades of gray. Wanting to be a better person does not mean separating ourselves from those who don't, or being critical of them. We all have similar struggles. The point here is not to condemn people who have significant flaws of character. To do so we may also have to condemn ourselves.

Is virtue boring?

Virtue is a word that has gone out of fashion in popular culture. We almost recoil at the sound of it. Many men think it sounds too feminine. However, the Latin root *vir* means "man." Our word *virility* comes from the same root. In other words, we ought to think of virtue as "manliness" or, to be more inclusive, as "strength."

The Greek word that is usually translated as "virtue" is *arête*. But more accurately it means "excellence," or being our best. Originally, virtue meant determination in the face of adversity and fortitude in doing our best in trying circumstances. Gradually other concepts such as honesty, self-control, kindness, humility, sensitivity, and generosity were associated with the idea of virtue, of becoming our best.

Reading a list of virtues, like those I just gave, may cause our minds to fuzz over, perhaps because we tend to be cynical about goodness. I saw a teenager recently wearing a T-shirt that said, "Everybody lies, no one minds." As sad as it is, there is an obvious truth written on his T-shirt for all to read. Leaders in whatever field we look at—politics, entertainment, sports, academics, business, the professions, and religion—have demonstrated the truth of it. They lie, and they often get away with it. The ethical pillars of human life and relationships have eroded, and if someone does appear to stand up for them, we are doubtful and tend to say, "Oh yeah? Let's wait and see."

If not simply a turnoff, virtue tends to be uninteresting to us. I read a list of some of the virtues I was talking about to a good friend, and she responded in mid-list with "Borrrring!" She is a good and decent person, but the words turned her off, as they do many of us. It is the literary critic's cliché that John Milton's *Paradise Lost* is much more interesting to us than his sequel, *Paradise Found*. The bad guys tend to fascinate us more than the good guys. Even Jane Austen said in a letter to her sister, "As you know, pictures of perfection make me sick and wicked."

Religion, virtue, and self-righteousness

Partly, virtue has become unpopular because of the decreasing centrality of either religion or spirituality in our lives. We have become a much more materialistic society with the loss of the kind of organizing belief system that religion or spirituality affords. We have nothing to tack the ideas of goodness onto, no organizing philosophy that raises up these values and says, "These are important, and here is why they are important." Once, the seven deadly sins were more than simply "bad." They were "sinful" and "deadly" because they violated the expectations of God for how people ought to behave. With the loss of God in our society, many of us have stopped seeing bad behavior as "sinful." This has had the effect of making such behavior less bad, less deadly. Without such a lofty context, it has become the common cynical perception, true or not, that "everyone does it, so why not me?"

> Being religious or spiritual does not guarantee that we will develop character and virtue.

Of course, religion, or belief in God, is not a requirement for being an ethical person. My atheist friends are some of the most honest and ethical people I know. They have worked hard at thinking out a basis for their beliefs, as all people, religious or not, must do. Many people simply do not think about these things in any depth. They are not required to by their parents or by their society.

On the other hand, being religious or spiritual does not guarantee that we will develop character and virtue. Ideally, religion and spirituality offer some central beliefs around which to develop our character and our understanding of goodness. Everyone, whether atheist, agnostic, or believer in any particular faith, has to do the hard work of putting together what "character and virtue" mean for them. And then they have to live it.

Here is an example of a man who could not really live his faith, and his failure had major consequences for his family. Caleb, a religious churchgoer, divorced his wife, May, after twenty-seven years of marriage when he was fifty. He had an excellent income and she got their very large and expensive house in the divorce settlement, but with no additional cash or alimony since their children were grown. In a classic midlife crisis, he had begun an affair with another woman and quickly married her after the divorce. Then, three years after this marriage, he died of a heart attack. He had made a new will and left everything he owned (which was more than he had disclosed in the divorce settlement) to his new wife. The old family of wife and three (adult) children was totally cut off, including from his pension benefits. They got nothing from his estate. They reminded me of the Dashwood women in *Sense and Sensibility* who, when Mr. Dashwood died, got nothing from his estate due to the inheritance laws in England at the time.

Severely upset about this, as well as by his death, all four of them came in for therapy. They were deeply angry with the new wife for "stealing him away," and for "stealing" what they thought of as their inheritance. Two of the children wanted to go after her in court even though a lawyer had told them they had no case. The third child, the oldest, said, "Look, there are no guarantees for anything in life. We don't know what it will bring us, ever. We can spend the next five years of our lives fighting this, or we can move on and deal with things as they are." Eventually her views prevailed.

The children's principal concern became their mother, May. She had no real skills for a career, having been a housewife all her adult life. They all pitched in financially to help her finish a college degree, and she ended up with a decent job and a pension. I spent a lot of time with her in therapy. Of course, part of what she wanted to do was look at what had happened in her marriage to Caleb. She began to see more clearly how her dependency on him over the years had become a drag for him. The woman he married after the divorce was a successful, more independent career woman, and May could see how he would be attracted to her. This, of course, did not excuse his behavior. He had other options for how to deal with her dependency.

Initially she hated being alone and on her own. While she had been an attractive, socially active young woman at the time of her marriage, she had never lived on her own or even made many of her own decisions. She went right from her own family, where she had been fairly dependent, to her marriage with Caleb. And he took charge there. Eventually she began to enjoy "having my own life and making my own decisions." She said, "I would hate to go back to the kind of life I had with Caleb. I like taking care of myself. I only wish I could have discovered this while I was still with him. We both would have been happier."

So May took responsibility for her part in the difficulties of the marriage, not that she "made" Caleb behave the way he did. He had his share of responsibility as well. She became a better person. They both brought emotional immaturities to the marriage and this produced a lack of goodness, in spite of the religious beliefs they both held.

After about four years of seeing May and her adult children in therapy (mostly individually), I had them all come together for a termination session. They all affirmed how they had grown and how their growth might not have happened if things had not gone as they did. Each one said some version of "Amazingly, I am a happier person now." I think they were also better people.

Unfortunately, many of the people who talk about virtue today tend to have a kind of self-righteous, moralistic approach to life that most of us are turned off by. There had been some of this quality in Caleb, and I am sure he was confused by his own actions. They may be priggish, stiff, humorless, arrogant, judgmental, unforgiving, and often unable to actually live the values they profess. Austen shows us plenty of such people in her novels. They are the ones who tend to think of themselves as, in her words, "pictures of perfection."

Most of us have known people who have presented themselves as virtuous, only to be revealed later behaving unvirtuously. Our hypocrisy-detectors are very sensitive, and they go on alert around anyone rumored to be "good." We have plenty of pretentious leaders who claim to be virtuous, including among the clergy. But they end up being revealed as self-centered and corrupt. The reality of hypocrisy, however, ought not to make us cynical. We need to promote virtue in relationships and in public life all the more fervently.

We need to continue to believe in the virtues, attempt to live them in action under the sometimes trying circumstances of our lives, and strive for the qualities of goodness that make for a happier relationship. Goodness can be interesting and appealing. Austen's novels demonstrate this. I see it as heroic to engage in the personal struggles involved in behaving well in relationships. May and her daughters demonstrated this. Virtue is about strength of character.

How did virtue become "bad"?

I partly blame my own field of psychotherapy for giving virtue a bad name. The decline of interest in developing our character and becoming more virtuous people almost exactly coincides with the growth of psychotherapy. Virtue began to get a bad reputation in Freud's time. Stated simplistically, he believed that an overly severe superego (the conscience) could lead to neurotic and psychotic patterns partly through the repression of one's deepest urges and feelings. Thus a focus on the exploration and verbal expression of our underlying repressed urges and feelings and our emotional wants in relationships, rather than the development of character traits, became the focus of psychotherapy. Gradually, among his followers, an emphasis on virtue was seen to be a restrictive route followed by the repressive conscience of an overactive superego.

Modern therapists have also tended to emphasize underlying feelings more than thinking and behavior. All three are important, but we have encouraged clients to go deeper into their feelings and often ignored the clients' ability to think about, for example, the particular values they want to uphold in their lives and behavior. Sometimes it seems that being a decent human being has taken a backseat to "honestly" expressing feelings. In addition, our emotional wants from others, like our partners, have superseded a focus on how *we* are with them.

Many psychotherapists, in a desire to promote good relationships, have tried to promote a "scientifically based, value-free" approach to therapy. As a profession, generally, we have failed to understand that any kind of therapeutic intervention will represent and promote some kind of value.

Having a "feeling focus" is a good way to avoid the question of our own goodness.

Therapy cannot be "value-free." To live and to act is always to choose one value, one belief about what is important, over another. We are always expressing our values in our actions. As a consequence of this recognition, some marriage and family therapists are beginning to pay attention to the importance of character and values in making better relationships.

Some therapists now recognize that the specific skills they may wish clients to develop for bettering their relationships require emotional maturity to implement them consistently. Knowing how to engage in good communication skills is one thing. The skills are relatively easy to learn. But being able to use them in a respectful way in the midst of a heated discussion with your partner, a family member, a friend, or a coworker is quite another thing. That requires more than the technical knowledge of the skills; it requires maturity.

Feelings and virtue

Many relationship therapists try to get couples to identify and express their feelings to one another. I agree that it is generally better to know what we are feeling than not. Getting clearer about feelings often helps us to get clearer about what we do and don't want from our partner. But here is the rub. These feelings and wants are usually other-focused; they are *reactive*. Having a "feeling focus" is a good way to avoid the question of our own goodness. Often in relationships, if we are not trying to please our partner, then we are trying to get our partner to please us. This focus on feelings takes the focus off issues of our own virtue. What kind of person do I want to be? What kind of a partner do I want to be? What is *my* (not my partner's) definition of what it means to be good to my partner, and good for my partner, as well as for me?

One husband in marital therapy came in with a long list of complaints about his wife, Joy. Stan was angry with her and saw her as uncaring. His biggest complaint was her distance and coolness toward him. After he went through his list, I could have turned to her and asked, "What are you feeling as you listen to your husband's complaints?" But I saw this as unhelpful. I knew she was sitting there full of angry resentment. If she had been willing to open up, she would have said something like she felt "angry" and "hurt," and probably she then would have attacked him for how he was toward her. Then he would have reacted to her and they would have, right there in my office, the same fight they have at home, ending with lots of distance.

Instead, I said to Stan that his complaints showed me that he cared about the relationship and wanted to be closer to his wife. I asked why he thought Joy was not responding more to his desire to be closer to her. He responded with theories about her as a person. I asked him what he thought would be most difficult about living with *him*; what about *him* might explain her distance from him? This stopped him and he was quiet for a while, struggling to think. But then he started on her again. Interrupting him, I said that it was interesting that when I asked about him, he wanted to tell me more about her.

Gradually, as we talked, he was able to focus more clearly on himself and saw that a complaining husband would more likely get distance from a partner than closeness. I asked him if he was being the kind of person he would like to be with her. He said no. "Well, what can you do about that?" I asked. He got the point and we spent quite a bit of time talking about how he was with her and what he would like to do instead. When I turned to Joy, I steered her away from this discussion and asked her about her life as a child growing up in her family and, in particular, about her relationship to her father. She revealed a pattern of dealing with him, when he complained about her, much like she did with Stan. We pursued this later in the therapy.

At the next session, Stan said, "Well, I don't know why I am surprised about how good things have been. I surely know the way this works at the office; I just didn't apply it to my own marriage." Stan developed his emotional maturity further through a growing self-knowledge. His willingness to look at himself and how he was behaving in the marriage allowed him to then think about how he wanted to be. First, he became more aware of his own functioning and the impact of that on his wife. This willingness to look at himself took a certain amount of strength. Then he was able to start working at changing. This did not address all their issues, but it gave both of them a new way to work at it and make progress on the tough stuff they both had to deal with.

The point of feelings is primarily to provide us with information about ourselves within our emotional context. But this should then lead us to think about how we want to behave with others. This usually does not happen; instead, like Stan, we stay focused on others. Our feelings tend to be a part of our reaction to others and how we think they are with us. In short, we are negatively other-focused.

This feeling-based other-focus keeps us in the role of victim. Stan believed he was the victim of Joy's distance and what seemed to him to be her "recalcitrance." She believed, in her anger and resentment at him for his criticism, that she was a victim of his attacks. Both, in a sense, felt harmed by the other, although they dealt with it differently. When they both were more able to focus on their own actions in the marriage and stop "feeling like a victim" of the other, they started doing better.

We generally feel happy when others are the way we want them to be with us, and unhappy when they are not. With this kind of focus, a lot of our energy then goes into trying to get others to be the way we want. And then they react to how we are trying to change them, like Joy keeping her distance from Stan. Then we react to their reaction and it is off to the races. This effort is both a frustrating and normally a losing battle; it keeps us unhappy and stuck, and feeling like a victim of the other's bad behavior.

Virtue is about living one's life by principle and implementing those principles in our everyday relationships, even when we do not "feel" like it. It is about making moment-to-moment decisions in our relationships that allow us to be true to what we profess and believe without being demanding or moralistic with others about how they "should be." It requires knowing ourselves and being clear about the kind of character we want to build for ourselves. It requires a focus on how *we* are doing at living a good life, not a focus on others and how they are presumed to be failing. It makes a project out of changing self rather than trying to change others. This is the primary prerequisite for having a good relationship. It is the way to create a happy, satisfying, and fulfilling life.

❦ FOUR ❧

WHY WE FAIL TO DO GOOD

Goodness, ignorance, and thoughtlessness

What keeps us from doing the good we profess to believe in, particularly in our close relationships? Christians might answer this question by saying it is sin. This answer, however, does not take us very far in knowing what specifically to do about it. Most of us believe, for example, that it is important to be kind, considerate, and loving in our relationships. Some of us do a better job than others at achieving these goals. Most of us fall short more often than we like to admit.

To some extent, we fail to do good out of ignorance; we simply don't know better. Normally this lack of knowledge is only a fault of youth or lack of training. We get better with age and experience. In Jane Austen's novels, Catherine Morland (*Northanger Abbey*), Fanny Price (*Mansfield Park*), and Emma Woodhouse (*Emma*) each need to be mentored, in varying degrees, in the ways of goodness. These young women are simply ignorant and need help learning how to be better. They gradually overcome their ignorance. Other Austen heroes have a greater understanding at the beginning of their stories and have learned most of the skills they need, although they struggle with doing what they know they need to do to be better. All of them face continued tests of their character, are threatened with several kinds of loss, and have to draw upon their emotional maturity to move ahead in life.

> We often know the right thing to do and still fail to do it.

Or we may fail to do good out of simple thoughtlessness. A man at a party, enjoying innocent flirting with a female friend, may not be aware of the impact on his wife. A woman at the same party may so much enjoy her own witty repartee that she misses the fact that she has just verbally cut another person and essentially made fun of her. When the impact of their behavior is pointed out to these two, they are ashamed and apologize for their thoughtlessness.

Anxiety as a sense of threat

Mostly, however, we fail to act correctly because of our anxiety. Anxiety is one of the most common and powerful experiences we have, usually on a daily basis. Most of us are neither evil people nor highly disturbed people for whom badness is deeply and integrally a part of who we are. But we often know the right thing to do and still fail to do it. We may have some degree of anxiety about a variety of things like acceptance and approval, money, status and recognition, or emotional security in a relationship. At a party, a man may brag about an accomplishment of his. He knows bragging is not a good thing, but he is anxious to be accepted and well thought of by others, so he does it.

Each area of anxiety, to the extent that we are not getting what we want, or are getting what we do not want, represents a kind of emotional threat. The threat may be experienced as a possible loss, for example, loss of money, loss of status, loss of a partner, or loss of closeness. The possibility may be only an imagined worry about the future, but that does not make it any less threatening. The bragging man fears a loss of acceptance and this feels threatening to his emotional well-being. The anxiety about the loss, real or not, can lead us to behave in self-centered ways in the mistaken belief that doing so will make us feel more secure or increase the chances that we will get what we want.

For example, a wife expects her husband to look at her and pay attention to her when she tells him about something that was upsetting to her that day. Instead, he continues to read the paper while she talks, making a kind of "uh-huh" sound. He misses the point of what she is saying. Consequently, she feels unimportant to him and uncared for. The first ten times this happens, she may give up and walk away in silence, quietly stewing. Then, on the eleventh time, she blows up. He wonders what has happened and sits up and pays attention. Over time she discovers that the only way she can get his attention is to blow up, and this becomes a pattern for them. But eventually he pays less attention even to her blow-ups.

This loss of his attention is a threat to her, in the sense that she fears never having the kind of friendship she wants to have with her husband. It may become a sort of threat for him as well as he becomes uncomfortable with her blow-ups over what he considers to be petty issues. He starts to keep his distance even more and is less available to her. Her sense of threat grows. She is feeling the loss of the companionship in marriage that she deeply wants. This is what she got married for and she doesn't have it. Eventually, after years of attempting to get this companionship from her husband, she decides to leave the marriage. When she tells him this he panics, says he didn't know it was that important to her, and begs, "Please don't leave. I will do anything you want." Now he is deeply threatened by the possibility of losing her.

When any sort of emotional or physical threat appears, we quite naturally seek greater security. Here is another way the scenario above could play out. When she is angry with him, he may offer a list of excuses or defenses for why he did what he did, or he may go on the counterattack and blame her. Or he could go quiet, withdraw, and not only refuse to talk about it, but leave the house and stay out all night. All of these may be security operations on his part, trying to make himself feel safer by "getting her off my back." She won't have a sense of this and will simply take it as a lack of love on his part. If she fears the aloneness of being divorced, then she may do whatever she can to not make waves and keep the peace. She may be tempted to comply with anything he wishes, or even to compromise her beliefs and values to feel more accepted and secure in the relationship. She will do anything not to lose him.

This giving up of self is another strategy we may use to allay the possible threat. The wife may think, "If I just don't push who I am, or what I want, then he will stay with me." People in close relationships may do small versions of this on a regular basis without much real damage to self being done. But when it becomes a regular pattern over time, with significant losses of self, then depression is the likely result. This is a price many are willing to pay to gain some sense of security in a relationship.

The more emotionally mature we are, the stronger is our own sense of inner safety and security so that in uncertain and insecure circumstances (like an angry or an unresponsive partner) we do not compromise self out of fear. We can act simply on the basis of what makes sense, without being defensive or aggressive. Or if we know we have behaved inappropriately, we can listen to our partner's complaints, how he or she was affected by our behavior, apologize, and start behaving differently. This is part of what I mean by goodness or emotional maturity; it is the ability to remain true to our principles in the midst of anxious experiences without needing to react inappropriately to the possible threat.

> Anxiety is the primary complicating factor affecting our level of emotional maturity.

Or, put another way, we know what is truly threatening and what is not. Unless our partner has a knife or a gun or is swinging fists, there is not much real threat in anger itself. Whatever threat we experience is usually imagined. We add something to the anger that makes it into something worse and more threatening. And this anxiety causes us to act in self-protective and usually inappropriate ways.

I grew up without much anger directed at me as a child. I lived only with my mother, and she was quite accepting and undemanding of me. So, as an adult, I didn't have much experience with anger aimed at me. In premarital counseling, the pastor asked Lois and me, "What do you two fight about?" I naively said, "Fight? We don't fight; we love each other." When we then got married and Lois was occasionally angry with me (usually quite appropriately), I got very scared (threatened) and handled this by shutting down emotionally and distancing. In my anxiety I made it into a bigger deal than it was, and then I responded inappropriately. This only made things worse.

Anxiety is the primary complicating factor affecting our level of emotional maturity. It was at the core of nearly every clinical situation I worked with. The more we are affected by it, the less able we are to function in an emotionally mature manner. The two are mutually incompatible. An extreme example would be men who batter their wives. Only a handful of these men are true sociopaths who consciously use violence to intimidate without any sense of anxiety or a bad conscience.

Most battering men are indeed quite anxious and insecure. Their violence is a cover for this. They believe that controlling their partner and her behavior will bring them a greater sense of emotional comfort and reduce their sense of threat, whatever the source. Whenever they realize how badly they have behaved, they usually genuinely apologize. The apology, however, does not change them. When they next feel anxious they will again strike out and perhaps do serious damage to their partner. This is a common cycle in battering relationships.

The more anxious or insecure we are in general, the more likely we are to behave foolishly or badly. Anxiety interferes with our ability to think clearly; it narrows our focus and tends to support our automatic, reactive responses in difficult situations. Under the influence of anxiety, we might respond with paralyzing fear or we might attack in anger. Anxiety can also inspire reactions like ignoring, withdrawing, avoiding, getting defensive, or rebelling against someone who wants us to be a certain way.

The real or imagined threat may be to who we are as a self, to our personal integrity, our goals in life, the values we cherish, the relationships we have or want, our reputation, or even more basically, our ability to survive. Of course, the threat to self can be experienced in response to real physical dangers, such as accidents or illness. For example, it is quite normal for parents to want to strike out against a drunk driver who has injured or killed their child. But the imagined (not real) loss of a child to a drunk driver can bring on a nearly similar reaction in some people.

> Good, mature human beings have as strong a commitment to the well-being of others as they do to themselves.

Anxiety and self-centeredness

We all start off as children with a significant amount of selfishness and self-centeredness. Over the years of growing up, parents and teachers train us to be less this way and to be more considerate of others. Most of us learn this is a good way to be because it makes better relationships possible. But we never fully lose this self-centeredness, and in times of greater anxiety we become focused on looking out for ourselves, protecting ourselves from any sense of threat that might, in a very broad sense, bring damage to us. This is usually the basis of our selfish behavior.

Self-centeredness has a positive side. We have a responsibility to protect and look out for ourselves. We will be no good to anyone if we don't maintain our own life and integrity. Jesus said we are to love others *as* we love ourselves. This command assumes a natural love of self that looks out for our own well-being. We are asked, however, to be as invested in looking out for the well-being of others as we are for ourselves. It takes an emotionally mature person to be able to do this.

Good, mature human beings have as strong a commitment to the well-being of others as they do to themselves. They think about and attempt to bring about what is good for the whole group they are a part of, as well as what is good for themselves. This, of course, can be tricky business, since what we do to and for others (because it will be "good for them") is often done out of our own selfish desires and wishes. These "acts of kindness" for or to others can really be done out of our own self-centeredness. They can be about what will make *us* happy, or feel less threatened, more comfortable, safe, better about ourselves, or whatever.

Good parenting represents a mature commitment to children. The parent is concerned for the well-being of the child. But parents can have mixed motives in their actions for their children. I have worked with a fair number of adults who were sent to boarding schools when they were young. Their parents told them it was so they could get a good education. But the children had a very clear sense that the parents just wanted them "out of the way." On the other hand, some parents who homeschool their children, for example, may not really be thinking about what is best for their children. They may be dangerously "child-focused," in the sense that their child is their whole life and they need their child close by to feel good about themselves. They don't want to let them go. Being a parent is the primary way they feel good about self.

Sir Thomas Bertram, at the end of Austen's *Mansfield Park* (chapter 48), has to reflect on his failures as a father. He discovers many. One has to do with allowing his daughter Maria to marry a man he was sure at the time she did not love. Mr. Rushworth was very wealthy and Sir Thomas was impressed with this, even though he knew the man was a fool. His "selfishness" and what are later called his "mercenary" attitudes took over. He was not thinking about what was good for his daughter, but how her marriage to a wealthy man would look in the community, which valued having daughters marry wealthy men, even at the expense of their own happiness.

> Sir Thomas, poor Sir Thomas, a parent, and conscious of errors in his own conduct as a parent, was the longest to suffer. He felt that he ought not to have allowed the marriage; that his daughter's sentiments had been sufficiently known to him to render him culpable in authorizing it; that in so doing he had sacrificed the right to the expedient, and been governed by motives of selfishness and worldly wisdom.

Insecurity and reactivity

We all understand what it is to feel insecure in life and in relationships. Many of the couples I worked with often came in with the fear of losing their partner, or they may already have lost the partner in a divorce. In addition, other forms of loss may have threatened them: loss of job and income, loss of position or standing in the community, loss of a child or other important family member, or loss of a place they have lived. There are many forms of loss, and these can inspire a sense of insecurity or threat to our well-being.

The mother and her three daughters I mentioned in the previous chapter experienced a number of losses that they believed were threatening to their well-being. As it turned out, they were not really threatened, even though there was actual material loss for all of them. They learned that, in a number of ways, the losses were sad, but not a threat. While they were still experiencing the losses as a threat, they wanted to retaliate and try to remove the threat in that way. Their anxiety would have swept them up into a vortex of anger, attack, and battles that would have kept them anxious for many years and would not really have addressed the losses

By the end of Mansfield Park, *Sir Thomas has learned that by allowing his daughter to marry a man she did not love, for reasons of his own self-absorbed and "mercenary" attitudes, he had deeply harmed her. For very selfish reasons he had "sacrificed the right to the expedient."*

As Jane Austen's characters demonstrate, it is often difficult to distinguish between legitimate self-interest and selfishness, and it is all too easy to deceive ourselves into believing that we are doing what is right when in fact we are sacrificing the right for what is expedient for ourselves.

- *What steps might you take to guard against the tendency toward self-deception when it comes to judging the motives for your behavior in your relationships?*

- *In what ways might acting out of regard for the other's well-being rather than merely out of self-regard contribute to real happiness?*

they felt or given them a new direction in life. They would simply be stuck in time, reacting to Caleb's bad behavior.

People may feel uneasy about being who they are, or about saying to an emotionally important other person what they truly believe, or feel, or have done, out of fear of losing that important relationship. So they lie or cover up who they are. They may feel shame. Our insecurity can keep us from being a solid self in our relationships. This anxiety is the major reason people hide themselves in relationships, or develop "false selves" that are pleasing to others and conform to what others want of them. Some people are like chameleons, changing themselves to fit in with whomever they are with, like the character Zelig in Woody Allen's movie of that name. We can be articulate, well informed, and intelligent, as he was, and still hide who we really are. Intelligence and competence do not protect us from anxiety.

Most often, we hide ourselves out of a fear of rejection. We want to hang on to the relationship and be well thought of. But hiding is an automatic break in a relationship; it introduces distance. Remember Adam and Eve hiding from God in the Garden of Eden? The relationship was broken and that led to more lying and dissimulation. As many U.S. presidents and other politicians have discovered, breaking a moral code is one thing; covering it up and trying to hide it is something more significant.

Rather than lying and trying to fit in, others may become aggressive and go on the attack. We may be easily conflicted with whoever rubs us the wrong way or has expectations of us to be some other way than we are. What is less obvious is that these angry people are also functioning out of anxiety.

Anger is often a protective effort, covering the underlying fear of hurt that one might experience in a relationship. Often people who regularly experience hurt and disappointment, probably starting with their family life, are always on guard and ready to attack at the slightest sign of possible disappointment. Or anger can be just an anxious, self-centered reaction out of a sense of being affronted that others do not see things, or do things, the way we do. Or we may be so fearful of losing self to others by going along with what they want that we often rebel against them. Hiding behind bristling anger can be a very vulnerable and insecure person.

A father of three adult children came in to see me saying he needed help in knowing how to respond to an upsetting letter from his youngest son, who had remained distant from him for many years. The letter was highly critical of the father and recorded how inadequate a father he had been over the years of growing up. I asked him what his reaction to the letter was and he said, "I am very angry." As we talked about that reaction, he began to speak of the hurt he felt behind the anger.

I asked him to be as objective as possible and to tell me, from that perspective, what he thought of his son's evaluation of him as a father. After a moment of reflection, he said, "Well, he's right. I was a terrible dad while the boys were growing up, and my youngest son saw even less of me than the older boys did. I wasn't getting along with their mother, and I guess I just stayed away from home as much as I could. I didn't want to be around her." I was impressed with his ability to get some distance from his angry reaction and to gain a more objective perspective on his own behavior. It showed a certain amount of emotional maturity. We talked more about all of that and then I said, "What would it be like for you to put these kinds of things in a letter to your son and admit that he is right?" He said he would give it a shot and agreed to bring his effort in the next time for us to talk about.

> Emotional distance is a common mechanism we all use, at some point, in nearly all of our close relationships.

He brought the letter to our next session and we fine-tuned it some. It was a good letter. Not defensive. He owned up to his inadequacies, apologized, didn't blame his wife or anyone else, and said he understood his son's anger. He said he would like to have a better relationship with his son now. His son was impressed with the letter and said, "Well, if that really is what you think and want, then maybe we can get together. I would sure like for my kids to know their granddad." And he invited his dad to come for a visit. I talked with the father about how he would behave during the visit, and he prepared for several possibilities. Afterward we got together again and the father reported that "it was a wonderful visit." The last I heard he was connecting better with all of his sons and their families and he was deeply grateful that they had given him the opportunity to do this.

This father was able to drop his angry cover and own up to his mistakes. He was able to stop reacting and be more the way he wanted to be. He became a better person and they all became a better family. He displayed a maturity that not every father would have in this situation. He could just as easily have justified himself, saying something like, "You think I was a bad father? Well, you were all terrible children, and I didn't want anything to do with you. I still don't, so I don't ever want to hear from you again, or at least not until you apologize." I have known fathers who have reacted to their adult children's accusations in this way.

Anxiety and distance

The most common way of controlling anxiety within self, and protecting ourselves from a sense of threat, is to emotionally distance ourselves for some period of time from those people and situations we find anxiety provoking, like the father and husband in the example above. Most of us learn early in life that we can feel better and more comfortable if we just get away from whatever we think is upsetting us. If we can't get away physically, then we do it mentally. Emotional distance is a common mechanism we all use, at some point, in nearly all of our close relationships. When we become uneasy, or don't want to talk about something or do something with the other, we may often move away and be less available emotionally if not physically.

Nearly all of us want time alone (how much varies from person to person), but this is not the same as emotional distancing. Distancing is about reducing our anxiety when there is some kind of difficulty in a relationship. Teenagers slam their doors on their parents when told they can't do something they want to do. Wives and husbands shut up and withdraw from each other, or change the subject, or get interested in something else (work, hobby, church, or some activity they enjoy) or someone else (a friend, a social club, an affair partner). They spend less time being open with one another and perhaps act as if things are normal. This is primarily about trying to get some comfort for self by getting away from whatever is the source of the anxiety.

There is a way of taking time alone and withdrawing for the purpose of being able to reconnect in a better way. We may take time by ourselves to think through the issues involved, and then to think about how we want to be. In thinking about how I wanted to manage myself when my wife was angry with me, I constantly had to remind myself that this was normal in most relationships; it was just a new thing for me. I had to tell myself that this doesn't mean she hates me, is going to leave me, or wants to kill me (which, I have to admit, is where my fears sometimes went; it was that terrifying for me), and that this was not the most terrible thing in the world. It just meant that she was not happy about something I had done, or (more often) not done. Period. It was nothing to get myself all anxious about. And then I thought that I needed to be able to talk with her, keep myself calm while doing so, and come to some agreement with her about the issue. So I had to think about the issue itself and what my own position was. That was the easy part. The difficult part was keeping my inner sense of calm and ease while talking with her about our different perspectives.

As we mature, we have a greater ability to develop that inner sense of comfort and to bring it with us back into our relationships and into the events of our lives. We do not have to withdraw as much. We can be clearer about the issues themselves. True emotional maturity is the ability to be in the midst of an anxious relationship situation, or an upset group of people, and be emotionally connected with each person while not being run by either their anxiety or ours. The ability to stay focused on how we want to be and to have an inner calmness while actively relating to everyone involved is true emotional maturity. It is very difficult to stay in this place consistently without maturity.

Anxiety and money

Disagreement over money is the issue many couples bring in for counseling. Usually this is because there is either not enough of it, according to one of the partners, or one partner wants to do something different with it than the other partner. Money and its uses, for many of us, seem to go right to the heart of our sense of well-being and security. It is a highly symbolic issue and lots of anxiety can develop around it. This is the issue Lois and I began to contend with in the third year of marriage. I felt good about my money management skills since I was never in debt and never bought anything without cash in hand, in spite of being a very poor pastor at the time. But she didn't think I was doing well enough. I couldn't believe it. We were debt free. What more did she want?

She wanted to have a savings account. "A savings account!" I said. "What do we want that for?" I grew up with just my mother, who worked full time as a secretary from the time I was eight months old. I never heard her once mention anything about a savings account. Mostly she lived from paycheck to paycheck, and her own money rule was "Don't go into debt. Never buy on time." So I thought I was doing well. But in Lois's family saving money was an important thing to do. I was happy living paycheck to paycheck; that seemed normal to me. Lois was naturally anxious about having money for those "rainy days," something I didn't even consider possible. This issue took us a year to work through and lots of talking was involved. We had to sort through our values about what was important about money, and about having it. Eventually I began to see the light and we started a savings account.

Most of Austen's novels involve varying degrees of anxiety about financial security. Charlotte Lucas in *Pride and Prejudice* is a good example of the plight of many women in Austen's day. Charlotte was not likely to receive any proposals for marriage, having neither beauty nor wealth. So she literally "put herself in the way" of Rev. Collins, knowing he was looking for a wife. She knew he could provide the material security she would need after her father's death. Most women in Austen's day had no money of their own and were totally dependent on having a husband with an income.

At first, on hearing that Charlotte had accepted Rev. Collins's proposal, Elizabeth thought she could no longer be Charlotte's friend, since she considered him to be such a fool. Elizabeth lost respect for her; but after visiting the couple and seeing the kind of life Charlotte had been able to make for herself with a man she did not love, Elizabeth softened and accepted her and her choice for security. Many women through the ages have made Charlotte's choice. The recent fictional film about Jane Austen's life (*Becoming Jane*) does a good job of focusing on this issue and how important it was in her time.

Today, because more women are capable of being financially independent, the choice is often less necessary, but it has been a factor for some of my female clients. I have had a few clients who have made the choice to be married to a wealthy man they did not love or respect, or whom they really considered a fool. He was often willing to settle for this. But he also knew that her desire for financial security gave him the upper hand and that he could remain fairly inflexible on whatever changes she wanted.

To these couples, without being entirely specific about the issue, I said that I did not think I could do marital counseling with them, but if either one wanted to do any individual work with me, I would be willing to do that. Usually the woman would come in for a few sessions and we would have a frank discussion about what was going on. But it never went further than that. So many things were tied up in her need for having wealth as her primary security that nothing else took precedence. No other issues were allowed to intrude. The therapy did not proceed.

All of Austen's characters, even her heroes, want a certain amount of financial security. But her less emotionally mature characters are almost entirely focused on that and are willing to compromise their integrity to achieve it. They live as if financial security is the same as emotional security.

My female clients who married for money, and Austen's less exemplary characters like Lucy Steele (*Sense and Sensibility*), are not likely to experience the kind of satisfaction in life that most of us would expect. I suppose they would claim a kind of happiness that wealth can bring, in terms of material possessions, but it cannot be the happiness that is experienced by a good, mature person in a loving relationship.

FIVE

ANXIETY, CALMNESS, AND BEING A SELF

Awareness and anxiety

Very often the sense of threat that brings on our anxiety is not clearly defined, and we may not even be aware of feeling it. Our earliest experiences of anxiety occur before we are old enough to have the mental ability and words to organize and label our experience, like the infant who feels threatened and cries if Mother is not visible or close by. That is our automatic reaction. We often don't know how dependent we are on a relationship until it is at risk or disappears.

The bad or foolish characters in Austen's books, like Rev. Collins, Lady DeBourgh, and Mr. and Mrs. John Dashwood, do not subjectively think of themselves as anxious; they generally feel supremely confident and sure of themselves. And yet we can see, as more objective outsiders, how highly anxious they really are, and how their anxiety governs their lives and decision making. Their anxiety keeps them from doing the good they profess to believe in. They will do whatever they think is required to maintain their self-image (in terms of having a certain social status or economic security), whatever they believe is essential to who they are.

Rev. Collins, in *Pride and Prejudice*, has structured practically the whole of his life around having the good will of Lady Catherine DeBourgh. He is anxiously dependent on her and the support of her wealth. He needs to have her approval to feel secure within himself. He gives up his ability to think for himself. He thinks with her head. What she thinks and believes is what he thinks and believes.

Lady Catherine, on the other hand, appears to be an independent woman, needing no one. But in fact, she is highly dependent on being admired and respected by people in her own social circle, within which she considers herself a leader. How certain people think of her is more

45

important to her than being good. Wanting to be well thought of, she thrives on flattery and is dependent on having the people around her do what she wants them to do. Her desperate and unprincipled, authoritative effort to extort an agreement out of Elizabeth to not marry Darcy is an example of her anxiety at work. She thinks the name and estate of Pemberley will be "polluted" by a marriage of the Darcy name to the socially lower Bennets.

Many of Austen's wealthy characters are dependent on the concepts of status and class to bolster their sense of themselves. Sir Walter Eliot in *Persuasion* is a good example. He takes pride in his title and loves to read the *Baronetage of England*, which outlines the history of the upper classes, to confirm that he really is "in." The book gives him "occupation in an idle hour, and consolation in a distressed one."

Some people consciously feel threat in almost every aspect of their lives, even when there is no apparent danger. They do not normally feel safe except within the confines of their daily routine. Change of any sort can be threatening for them. Imagination can take over and create upset-

Many of Jane Austen's characters behave badly because they perceive (often falsely) much of what's going on around them as threats to their happiness. The resulting anxiety shapes (often unconsciously) their emotional and behavioral reaction to what's going on around them.

As Austen's characters demonstrate, anxiety-based behavior is often quite harmful to relationships. Ironically, behavior meant to reduce a perceived threat and relieve anxiety often has the opposite effect of strengthening the sense of threat and increasing anxiety.

- *To what degree do you consider yourself an anxious person?*

- *What, if any, threats do you perceive to your happiness and well-being?*

- *In what ways—for better or for ill—does the sense of threat and consequent anxiety shape your behavior and impact your relationships?*

ting scenarios. Even wealth does not protect them from this insecurity. In modern times Howard Hughes would be a good example.

Emma's fearful and hypochondriacal father, Mr. Woodhouse, is another good example. After his wife's death, he next has to endure the marriage and departure of his oldest daughter. Then comes the loss of Emma's governess, Miss Taylor, who was almost a part of the family, when she marries Mr. Weston. Austen lets us know early on what a major threat it would be to Emma's father if she were to marry and move away. In chapter 1 we read of Mr. Woodhouse:

> His spirits required support. He was a nervous man, easily depressed; fond of every body that he was used to, and hating to part with them; hating change of every kind. Matrimony, as the origin of change, was always disagreeable; and he was by no means yet reconciled to his own daughter's marrying, nor could ever speak of her but with compassion, though it had been entirely a match of affection, when he was now obliged to part with Miss Taylor too; and from his habits of gentle selfishness, and of being never able to suppose that other people could feel differently from himself, he was very much disposed to think Miss Taylor had done as sad a thing for herself as for them, and would have been a great deal happier if she had spent all the rest of her life at Hartfield.
>
> Emma smiled and chatted as cheerfully as she could, to keep him from such thoughts; but when tea came, it was impossible for him not to say exactly as he had said at dinner,
>
> "Poor Miss Taylor!—I wish she were here again. What a pity it is that Mr. Weston ever thought of her!"

His "gentle selfishness" is anxiety based. He lacks the goodness that goes with a mature character that can accept that others are different from him and want different things than what he wants. He prefers to think that everyone else is, or should be, the same as him, and should conform to his wants.

Our anxiety keeps us from doing the good we profess to believe in. We may do whatever we think is needed, in a self-centered way, to keep the sense of threat at bay, without realizing the bad behavior we are engaged in. One client never really "left home" when he got married. He had never lost his desire to please his mother and to have her continued love and support. Anytime he saw his wife as threatening the loss of his mother's approval and good graces, or interfering in his relationship with his mother, he attacked his wife and told her of her inadequacy. Out of her own anxious reasons, the wife went along with this behavior for many years until finally she had grown enough to say to herself (and him), "Who needs this? Let him live with his mother. I am better off on my own." Only then, under the actual threat of her leaving, did the husband realize that he really did want to be with his wife and begin to address his unresolved emotional attachment to his mother.

Slowly this husband became a more decent person in his marriage. He began to sort through the nature of his anxiety with his mother. He developed the ability to think for himself in relation to her and to be a self with her, openly saying what he thought. He had never really had this ability in relation to her. Her beliefs, thoughts, and wishes were dominant in his own mind, and he ran his life as if her head were screwed onto his shoulders. But he began to grow up, to mature in relation to her, and he began doing his own thinking.

His mother was indeed unhappy with this change. A real crisis developed in their relationship. She came in with him to several therapy sessions, and once she could move beyond her anger at him and his wife (who she thought was "the real problem"), she began to identify the sources of anxiety in her own life that had led her to want to keep her son so close. The son had always thought of her as a highly independent woman, strong, competent, secure, and certain about her beliefs. He had admired this and found her "solidity" reassuring. It was a new experience for him to begin to see both her anxiety and how it had affected her and her behavior with him. Insight into his compliant reaction to his mother's anxiety-driven behavior toward him led to real change.

In another case, a possessive widowed father (with overtones of Mr. Woodhouse) kept his nineteen-year-old daughter close to home and discouraged her from dating. He bought her all kinds of expensive things— like a new BMW convertible. As well as enjoying the benefits of his wealth, she genuinely loved her father and did not want to displease him. She felt sorrier for him around the loss of his wife than she did for herself over the loss of her mother. She claimed she felt stuck and controlled by what she knew to be his anxiety about being alone, but would feel guilty if she left him alone in order to develop her own social life. So she took on a quasi-housewife role with him, running the household, making meals, cleaning, and doing chores. She began to feel depressed, not quite realizing what it was about, and came in for therapy.

I was curious about her own compliance and lack of rebellion against her father's wishes. Slowly her social uncertainty emerged as a factor. Her mother had died early in her eleventh grade, and her life, instead of involving friends and boyfriends, became focused on her father and keeping things going at home. Her compliance with his wishes saved her from the normal anxieties every teen experiences around dating. She was attractive and boys did make overtures, but she rebuffed them.

In the course of therapy, I referred to Emma and her father. She read the book and liked it. She was taken with Austen's description of Mr. Woodhouse as a person of "gentle selfishness." She didn't think of her father as a bad person and this phrase helped. She also said she could identify with Emma's idea that she would never get married. I said, "Well, maybe in a sense you already are married." "Hmmm," she said. Although she said nothing more about it, this thought stuck with her. We also talked about Emma's lack of experience in love, and her real confusion as to what love was or what it would look like in a normal male/female relationship. She said there wasn't even a Mr. Knightley in her life, and I said that's great because he was so much older than Emma. (In my own private thinking I was aware that I could easily take on that role for her and I wanted to minimize that possibility as much as I could. I kept directing her to others, rather than me, for life advice.)

As she began reflecting on her own level of emotional maturity and took more responsibility for herself and her future, she got serious about going to college and becoming financially independent of her father. She began to be more active with old friends, went to some parties, and began to date. She needed to have a woman in her life whom she could talk with about these experiences, not just her few girlfriends. She had an aunt on her mother's side whom she liked and thought she could talk with, so I encouraged that. The aunt became a valuable resource for her in many ways. She could ask her aunt lots of questions about her mother (as well as her own life) because they had been close.

Her father began to have one health crisis after another (which seemed to require her to stay close), but the doctors could not diagnose any specific problems. I said, "Gee, he sounds just like Mr. Woodhouse." She got that, and struggled with the idea of leaving him alone in their home, but eventually she moved across town to a college dorm (with a couple of visits home during the week) for her first year of university.

Although her father came in for a few sessions, he refused to stay involved in therapy. Nevertheless, he slowly adjusted to his daughter's growing independence. He continued to have little sense of his own anxiety and how he behaved "badly" as a result. While he was materially generous, he was emotionally selfish. But his daughter more and more grew herself up and became a more mature person in her own right who still cared for her father. He became grateful for whatever he got of her attention and love.

But he never really got on with his own life independent of her while I knew them. At termination she said, "Well, he is free to run his life the way he wants, and so am I. What he does with his life is his job. It's not right that I keep doing what I have been doing." I just said, "Wow," and she smiled.

> When we fail to engage in developmentally and age-appropriate behavior out of anxiety, then we are wrong.

I liked that she used the concept of "rightness" in her comment. Many people would think that although her story was a sad one, she was doing right by looking after her father, and that she was a good girl. I think that when we fail to engage in developmentally and age-appropriate behavior out of anxiety, then we are wrong. There is an issue of goodness involved. Life involves development and change, and to hold these back is wrong. Her emotional maturity also showed in her lack of need for him to either change or approve of what she was doing before she could get on with her own life.

Change nearly always evokes some anxiety because it introduces us to the uncertainties of a new situation. We are all a bit like Mr. Woodhouse, who hates "change of every kind." Both my client and her father had their own anxieties stemming out of their mutual grief, which we did talk about when he came in with her. But they were ignoring how things had changed for them, not just through the wife/mother's death, but because of normal developmental changes. Their failure to think about and decide "What do I do now?" was, from my perspective, an issue of goodness.

Anxiety and becoming a solid self

When we are less anxious, we tend to react less, become calmer, and think more clearly. We are not so narrowly focused on one single issue and can see more of the factors involved in "the bigger picture." We then make better decisions. In the example above, this young woman's lowered anxiety about herself and her father allowed her to think more clearly about her own life, and what she did or didn't owe him. She had been giving up herself to him in order to keep him (and herself) calm and less anxious. Depression, which is one form of anxiety, is often about a giving up of self to someone else, or something else. As she reclaimed herself, her depression melted away. We rarely even talked about "the depression."

With our lowered level of anxiety, we can help others to calm down in relation to their anxiety, but in a way different from what she had been doing. She had been trying to calm him by being available to him. But instead, she learned that she did not have to do anything to or for him, or even tell him to "calm down." When one person in an emotional system can be calmer and more thoughtful, then others will begin to be calmer themselves. The daughter in this example did not tell her father that he was just being anxious and to calm down. She didn't try to diagnose his "problems," or try to convince him that he had a problem, or make him be different so then she could be "free." She just worked on changing herself. As she became calmer and more decisive about her life, his own level of anxiety eventually dropped to more manageable levels.

She became more focused on her own goals. She decided it was appropriate to be setting goals that involved her greater independence—going to school, developing a career, and becoming involved with age-appropriate men. As she did this, her father's anxiety initially went up and he had some apparent health symptoms. But we had discussed what possible reactions he might have and she was prepared for this and knew the challenge would be to maintain her own lower level of anxiety and her direction in life.

> Change happens in emotional systems when individual people work on becoming a more solid self in their relationships with others.

She was changing the balance in the relationship with him, and as a result, we had predicted that he would be more anxious. But she did not get caught up in changing her behavior so he would feel calmer and less anxious. With each health "crisis" phone call from him, rather than rushing home, she offered to call 911 for him and to have an ambulance sent. Calmly she stayed on her own course, did not get angry or upset with him, and initiated regular contact with him on her own schedule.

He slowly accepted that his anxious behavior was not going to dissuade her from pursuing her goals in life. So while he didn't actively pursue having his own life, he did get better simply because of her ability to better define herself and stay calm while also keeping more normal, age-appropriate father-daughter contact with him. Change happens in emotional systems when individual people work on becoming a more solid self in their relationships with others.

Anxiety is a communicable disease. Whole societies can be taken over by it in times of crisis. However, just as people can "catch" anxiety from each other, they can also catch greater calmness. In *Persuasion*, the Musgrove family experiences a major upset when the oldest son, the one who will inherit the estate and be the leader of the family, breaks his collarbone in an accident. They all fear for his life. But everyone is too anxious to function adequately except for Anne Elliot, who typifies the calm, less anxious presence within an upset emotional system. She was able to think about what needed doing. We read in chapter 7:

> His collar-bone was found to be dislocated, and such injury received in the back, as roused the most alarming ideas. It was an afternoon of distress, and Anne had every thing to do at once; the apothecary to send for, the father to have pursued and informed, the mother to support and keep from hysterics, the servants to control, the youngest child to banish, and the poor suffering one to attend and soothe; besides sending, as soon as she recollected it, proper notice to the other house, which brought her an accession rather of frightened, enquiring companions, than of very useful assistants.

When we are less anxious, we can react less and think more clearly. We help others to calm down in anxious situations, as Anne Elliot does, simply by virtue of our own calmness and competent functioning. Anne does not tell anyone to "be calm," but her calmness affects others. They eventually "catch" it. Also, the more mature we are, the less we are affected by the anxiety of others. We can go about doing what needs to be done rather than being caught up in or reacting to their anxiety. This is also the case with Anne. The emotional maturity of having a more solid, less threatened self allows us to tolerate the normal anxiety we feel in the occasional emergencies of life and in the difficult relationships we may have, while not being guided by that anxiety. We can maintain the functional stability to deal with "what is" rather than being caught up in fears of what "might be," or as Austen says, "the most alarming ideas."

Too often we try to deal with our anxiety by trying to get those around us who are also anxious to calm down. We may say things like, "You are making me upset. Calm down!" Or the daughter described above could have said to her father, "You are making me depressed." But this is not factually true. *We* do these things to ourselves. Yes, it is in response to the behavior of the other (she probably wouldn't have gotten depressed without his behavior), but our emotional experience and the way we behave in response to others are our responsibility. In the same vein, we can't make others less anxious. That is not within our power. But we can lower our own level of anxiety, and this often (not always and certainly not immediately) helps others to be less anxious.

We all have anxiety. The only people who don't are dead people. To be alive is to be anxious. To be more mature is not a matter of having no anxiety, but of being comfortable enough with it so that we can still function adequately and not be governed by it. In challenging situations less mature people focus on reducing their anxiety, often by having others be responsible for it (like the father keeping his daughter close) rather than dealing competently with the situation they face in the context of their life goals. Focus on anxiety often leads to behaving badly or, as with the Musgrove family, inadequately.

Fanny Price is Austen's most anxious hero. In the course of *Mansfield Park*, she never loses her anxiety, although over time its intensity does diminish significantly. Her story demonstrates that anxiety does not have to undercut living a principled life and being good. By virtue of her difficult family history and her uncertain and ill-defined connections with others in the Bertram household, she has to struggle with maintaining her poise and direction in life nearly every day. Even when she has done no wrong, she can still feel wrong. Even when she has been most caring and of use to everyone, she can still feel useless. Even when she is clearly the most worthy person in the story, she may still feel worthless.

While the household members are rehearsing a play that they ought not to be doing, there is a general anxiety in the group. But they project the cause of their uneasy feelings onto Fanny because of her refusal to act a role in the play. They make her the source of their discontent. But they seem to know, at some level, that they are wrong to perform this play since Sir Thomas is in danger while away on business in the Caribbean.

This knowledge becomes obvious when he unexpectedly returns. Because Fanny chooses to not participate in the play, she is pushed to the outside of the group, but she struggles to stay connected with them rather than distancing emotionally. One way she copes with anxiety is by trying to be useful to others. As we read in chapter 18:

> Many uncomfortable, anxious, apprehensive feelings she certainly had; but with all these, and other claims on her time and attention, she was as far from finding herself without employment or utility amongst them, as without a companion in uneasiness; quite as far from having no demand on her leisure as on her compassion. . . . She was occasionally useful to all; she was perhaps as much at peace as any.

Fanny does not have a solid, strong sense of self like Elizabeth or Elinor, but she has more than all of the other people in her story. The only difference between her and the others in her story is that her anxiety is closer to the surface and she can experience it more directly. This doesn't keep her from acting correctly. The others are much less aware of their own anxiety and have no direct access to it, but in different ways it runs their lives.

❦ Six ❦

Self-Knowledge, Happiness, and Character in Relationships

Character and predicting happiness

Do you know what will make you happy? We live much of our lives saying, "If only I could really have the love of that person," or "have children," or "get that job" or "that promotion," or "live in that house," or "have that car," or "win the lottery, then I could be happy."

The study of happiness is a major new field of study in psychology. I mentioned Dr. Martin Seligman's work in chapter 1. He and his colleagues have done a great deal of research on happiness. He wants psychology to focus on what it takes to live a good and satisfying life, not just the emotional problems of life. He calls it Positive Psychology. His research supports the argument of this book, that happy people are those who have developed their character and strive to be good people.

The psychologist Daniel Kahneman won the Nobel Memorial Prize in Economic Sciences in 2002 for his research about how people choose and make decisions. This research then led him to look at how well or poorly people were able to predict what would make them happy. His work shows that after getting the things that we think will make us happy, and after indeed experiencing a brief spurt in our level of happiness, which may last for as long as a year or two (at the most), we return to whatever level of happiness we had before we got the desired person or thing. Whatever positive feelings we do have are usually not as intense as we think they will be, and they don't last as long as we expected.

> Most of us are as happy as we are going to be unless we set out to change.

We overestimate what the fulfillment of a wish will do for us, in part because we don't realize what demands will be made as a result of having the wish fulfilled. Getting the things that we think will make us happy often requires us to change in some unexpected but significant ways. They come with requirements for us to adapt to new realities. Winning the lottery is one of the best examples of this.

We fail to recognize that happiness is not really about the external aspects of our lives, like what we have or even who we are within our relationships. We are still the same person after the wish is fulfilled. Happiness is a property of the self. It is about who we are, the kind of people we are. Of course, there are people who, for example, are happier when they are married, but the opposite is also true. The point is that it is a mistake to expect marriage to make us happy, even if we marry the person of our dreams. Generally those people who are happy in marriage were happy people to begin with before marriage. Happy marriages are formed by happy people.

Most of us are as happy as we are going to be unless we set out to change. The ancient philosophers like Aristotle are right; happiness is, first of all, about being a good person. They said being happy is inextricably tied in with virtue. They believed that successfully developing and strengthening our character would produce the most satisfaction in life. Those who have a weaker moral life are not as happy, no matter how successful they appear to be. They foolishly pursue wealth, status, security, and material things as a way to feel better about self, and it does not work. Of course, there are certain minimal wants and needs that make life more comfortable and secure. Seligman's group has arrived at having an income of $50,000 a year for North Americans. Up to this amount people are somewhat happier with an increased income. Above it their level of happiness hardly changes at all.

Self-knowledge and happiness

A basic attribute needed for becoming a better and happier person in life generally is self-knowledge. We all think we know ourselves, but that is a fallacy. It is not easy to know ourselves. It requires a great deal of objectivity. Self-knowledge, knowledge of others, and a correct understanding of the situation we are a part of or the context in which we live all go hand in hand. People of good character have a better grasp of these three areas than do others because their perceptions are more accurately based on reality.

So many of the clients I have worked with over the years have found that their predictions of what would make them happy were totally off base. One smart, attractive woman, Linda, kept falling for exciting guys who lived in the fast lane of life. Excitement was really her theme with men. Wealth was a secondary factor. After two failed marriages to men who fulfilled this wish, but who also abused her physically and emotionally, she decided that maybe she was doing something wrong and came in for therapy. During therapy we never discovered the basis of her desire for excitement. Nevertheless, she did decide to start giving a chance to the kind of men she had previously labeled "dull and boring."

We started talking about her life generally, apart from the men in her life. We looked at what she personally was interested in, quite apart from whether or not there would ever be another man in her life. We talked about what was important to her in life, what she valued the most, and what kind of person she wanted to be. She started to think about her life in terms that did not have to have a man as a central factor or focus for her. This was not easy for her. She did a lot of family work, spending more time with both her parents, separately as well as together. She spent more time talking with her sister as well.

She developed a much better relationship with each of these family members, especially with her father. She was amazed to find out more about his life as well as what kind of struggles both her parents had dealt with in their lives, growing up and as young adults. She had kept her distance from her family as an adult because she felt ashamed of them and their relatively poor, working-class background. She hadn't liked thinking of herself as a part of them. But gradually, as she listened to their stories, she found herself feeling prouder of them and how they had dealt with life. She began to own them as "my family" and a part of who she was. She found this was also affecting her own sense of herself.

Eventually she started dating some of the men she would not have given a second thought to before. After two years of dating, while getting to know her family and herself better and working at adjusting her attitudes and values, she found a man who was steady, reliable, caring, and interested in her. We terminated therapy at this point, but in rather short order, she married him, had two children, went back to school, got an interesting job, and found a happier life.

Several years later, I ran into her at the local supermarket, where she filled me in on these things and what she had learned about herself. She said to me, "You know, Ron, it really wasn't about the guys. It was about me and my family. I thought the guys would do something for me that I thought my family had not done for me. But really, no one could have done this for me. I really like my life right now. Tim and I are doing some really interesting things, and I have all the excitement I can handle. We are close to my parents as well as to his, and they all enjoy being grandparents. They helped a lot while I went back to school."

She said she was the happiest she has even been and this present marriage definitely helped. She also said (because I asked her) that it wasn't simply the marriage that made her happier. It was becoming a more mature and less emotionally dependent person. She said doing the family work in therapy was the most important thing she had ever done. It changed her sense of self. It wasn't just that she was closer to them, which she liked, but that she got a new sense of self out of doing it.

> Knowledge of ourselves and of our goals, beliefs, values, and how we actually behave in relationships is the key to becoming a happier person.

She felt like she had grown up into an adult who would be satisfied with her life even if she hadn't married. This is part of what I mean by virtue. She made better choices for living a better life—and she had learned a great deal about herself.

Knowledge of ourselves and of our goals, beliefs, values, and how we actually behave in relationships is the key to becoming a happier person. It took Linda some time to figure out that she thought of herself as inadequate, dull, and boring and that she thought she needed an exciting man in her life to make her different. These issues of self were all tied up with her sense of her family. As she overcame her childhood picture of them and established a more adult relationship with them, her sense of self changed as well. Once she began to clarify for herself what would be interesting and important for her, she went for it. And she had a more mature partner who supported her desire to do this.

To have a satisfying relationship, we must know what we bring (or don't) to the relationship. Jane Austen has one of her characters say words that really apply to Linda (and all of us). Edmund Bertram (in *Mansfield Park*) hopes, in his final parting words to Mary Crawford (a woman whom he had thought he loved), that she would "not owe the most valuable knowledge we could any of us acquire, the knowledge of ourselves and of our duty, to the lessons of affliction."

Emerson said, "What lies behind us and what lies in front of us pales in comparison to what lies within us." In our less mature moments, at difficult points in a relationship, we often choose to focus on how circumstances are against us, or on what others have done to us or may do to us later, or on what they haven't done for us, or on how the other is behaving badly, rather than on how we are behaving.

Self-knowledge is especially critical for discovering our faults and how we have behaved badly toward others. Linda became ashamed with how she had treated her family. It takes strength and courage to look at ourselves honestly. This is why I think that most of my clients have been courageous people; they have been willing to look at themselves and (sometimes with some necessary prodding from me) to focus on their own behavior rather than that of others. It takes character to recognize our own fallibility. This is also why many people avoid therapy.

So many of us think we are experts on the behavior of others—how they are failing or inadequate, and how they appear to negatively affect us. But we forget about how our own subjectivity may skew our perceptions, and we may ascribe to ourselves more insight and understanding than we really have. And then, even if someone has behaved badly with us, do we know what we may have done to inspire that behavior? I am not saying that we are responsible for their behavior, only asking that we consider our part in the overall emotional process.

Here is a personal example. Over the years I have learned how I can get a certain kind of reactive response from my wife, Lois. I used to think it was just her, leaving me out of the equation. When I got a reaction from her, I used to say, "What's up with you?" Partly this was accurate since I don't make her that way. But what is also true is that I play a part in that reaction. When anxious, I can get a certain kind of edge in my voice that makes my comments sound like a criticism or a demand. In my calmer moments I can ask myself, "What did I do to get that reaction?" Knowing my part in this means I can recognize what is going on with me ahead of time and change my behavior.

Lois could also work on her part in the process by looking at how she lets herself get triggered and figuring out how to change her reaction. In fact, she has done this. But whether she did or didn't isn't really the issue for me. I am responsible for my part and that is what I need to learn about and change. In couples therapy, my clients often looked at these kinds of interactive processes, what each person's part was, and how to modify them. But one doesn't really need to be in therapy to do this. People have been developing this sort of self-knowledge and ability to change since long before therapy existed.

Subjectivity and awareness

Self-knowledge requires awareness of how we are behaving. One of the problems with developing an accurate sense of ourselves is that we can so easily fool ourselves. We can imagine ourselves to be one kind of person when we are actually another. For example, we may think of ourselves as kind and generous when, in fact, we are in important ways mean, self-ish, and greedy. We do this by allowing our imagined picture of ourselves (what we want to believe about ourselves based on our subjectivity) to obliterate any knowledge of our actual behavior (the objective facts).

One well-known, modern confidence man from France, by the name of Rocancourt, was able to swindle many smart, wealthy people out of millions of dollars. He made more than $40 million before he was caught. Even though he was relatively young, he conned men and women on the French Riviera. In the United States he worked the Hamptons and Beverly Hills. He was finally caught in Whistler, British Columbia (a ski resort where big-money people hang out), where he was working his swindle.

In an interview years later after he got out of prison, he said, "Look, I was able to do what I did only because these wealthy people were greedy. I told them that within months I could get them a 500 percent return on the money they gave me, and they went for it." He took the money they gave him and lived like a Rockefeller, which was the family name he was using. His lavish lifestyle was the only thing that convinced people that he was legitimate. The targets' greed blinded them to the clear truth about this man and led them to ignore things about him they could have easily checked.

We often make assumptions about the person we have fallen in love with, without really knowing them.

Many of the people who were conned were probably proud of their ability to be a judge of character, and they had full confidence in their own sense of themselves in this area. And they probably didn't even think of themselves as greedy. Imagine how foolish they had to feel when the truth came out. Rocancourt said he flattered them, telling them they were smart and were making a good decision. They chose to believe him. This is sub-jectivity at work. This is lack of knowledge of self and a too-trusting atti-tude toward their own abilities. Hopefully they learned some things about themselves in this expensive lesson and didn't just get angry at Rocancourt and blame him. They participated in the swindle.

Many a person has wrongly trusted his or her own intuition in mat-ters of love, not really knowing his or her self. We often make assumptions about the person we have fallen in love with, without really knowing him or her. And when it all falls apart, we say he or she "tricked" us, rather than admitting, "I failed to pay better attention to what was going on in front of me. If I had looked, the evidence was there. But I chose to believe my wishes, wants, and hopes rather than dealing with the reality of the person's behavior. It was all there and I chose not to see it." I heard things like this over and over in my clinical practice.

In Austen's book *Pride and Prejudice*, the main hero, Elizabeth Bennet, has a dramatic moment of self-discovery that many of us could iden-tify with. She chooses to believe a relationship con man by the name of Wickham, who flatters her with his attentions. He is considered a "good catch" by many women because he has many outstanding attributes. He tells her an untrue story about Darcy, his rival for winning her affections, and she chooses to believe him partly because she has her own prejudi-cial attitudes toward Darcy. When the truth finally comes out in a clarify-ing letter from Darcy, Elizabeth is totally undone. But she doesn't blame Wickham as much as she does herself. This is a sign of her courageous maturity.

Darcy's letter forces Elizabeth to think through one encounter after another with each of them, seeing the factors that were present but that she had missed at each point in time. Why had she missed them? Because her feelings, her subjective experience at the time—the flattery of receiving a handsome and charming man's attention, and her negative stance against Darcy because of his rude behavior toward her early on—kept her from seeing all that was going on. She knows that the issue is neither Darcy nor Wickham, but her own immature self that chose to believe one and not the other in spite of the evidence in front of her. Her vaunted pride of dis-cernment had been subverted by her vanity and prejudice, and she didn't know it. In chapter 18, as she reflects on Darcy's letter, we read:

She grew absolutely ashamed of herself. Of neither Darcy nor Wickham could she think, without feeling that she had been blind, partial, prejudiced, absurd.

"How despicably have I acted!" she cried. "I, who have prided myself on my discernment! I, who have valued myself on my abilities! who have often disdained the generous candour of my sister, and gratified my vanity, in useless or blameable distrust. How humiliating is this discovery! Yet, how just a humiliation! Had I been in love, I could not have been more wretchedly blind. But vanity, not love, has been my folly. Pleased with the preference of one, and offended by the neglect of the other, on the very beginning of our acquaintance, I have courted prepossession and ignorance, and driven reason away, where either were concerned. Till this moment, I never knew myself."

Elizabeth gets it—this is a matter of self-knowledge. Being more objective about ourselves and how we function will lead us to greater clarity in understanding others and how they function in relationships. This inevitably makes for better relationships.

Imagination and reality

Part of the experience of falling in love involves, as Elizabeth says, a kind of blindness. We are taken over by a kind of fever (due to hormones mostly) and we imagine we know the other person. This nearly always leads to surprises later on. The people who feel hurt by the surprises often blame the other person for deceiving or tricking them, rather than looking at themselves. Some people become cynical and say, "You can't trust anyone." Part of what can be wonderful about becoming closely involved with another is that, along with getting to know another person, we are given the opportunity to learn about ourselves and how we function.

Molly was typical of many of my clients, men as well as women. She told me how much she had been in love with Jim before they got married and how wonderful he was to her. She said, "He really seemed to be the man of my dreams. But one of my girlfriends kept asking me how well I knew him. I dismissed her, saying I know him perfectly well." She admitted that she had noticed he occasionally drank too much, but she thought that was just because he had come out of a previous unhappy relationship in which he had been "treated like dirt." She knew she could make a difference in his life and that they would be happy together.

Two years later the marriage was over. She came in to see me after many drunken episodes and "flings," which he claimed were "just sex." He had left her for another woman. She was devastated and went into a real slump. In therapy, however, the issue she wanted to look at (quite correctly) was not "What made him that way? Why didn't he love me?" Rather, what she wanted to understand was "Why did I act that way? Can I ever trust myself to know a man and choose wisely?"

Her focus in our work was on self-knowledge, a positive sign for her growth. She took some time to sort through her part in the courtship and marriage with Jim. Then as she started dating again, we talked about how she was managing herself, how her values played out in her relationships, and how she was going about getting to know the men. She found the whole thing "fascinating." A couple of years later, after becoming a different person in her relationships, she made a good marriage to a man who loved her and treated her well.

Today we speak of people being "in denial," unaware of their own behavior, intent, and experience. Among Austen's novels, *Emma* is a good example. Emma considers herself to be an expert on others; however, her lack of self-knowledge keeps her from knowing them. She is caught up in her own subjectivity and imagination and cannot see this. Because of her inability to know herself, she is capable of doing real damage to others in her community—to Harriet Smith, Miss Bates, Jane Fairfax, and others. And in matters of love, she is ignorant of her own heart.

As the conclusion of the novel draws near (chapter 47), Emma begins a series of reflections on her own self-deceptions and her lack of understanding of both herself and others. Preferring her own imagined beliefs to the reality of who others are, and the wrong assumptions as to what she could do in relation to them, she is blind to her blunders and foolish actions. The italics are mine.

> The rest of the day, the following night, were hardly enough for her thoughts. She was bewildered amidst the confusion of all that had rushed on her within the last few hours. Every moment had brought a fresh surprise; and every surprise must be matter of humiliation to her. How to understand it all! *How to understand the deceptions she had been thus practicing on herself,* and living under!

The blunders, the blindness of her own head and heart! . . . She saw, that in persuading herself, in fancying, in acting to the contrary, she had been entirely under a delusion, totally ignorant of her own heart.

We get clues about who we are and gain self-knowledge by paying attention to our behavior in relationships. In doing this we have to be as objective as we possibly can about ourselves. If we deny our part in rela-

We can train ourselves to behave differently in emotionally upsetting critical situations.

tionship difficulties, we lose access to knowing more about who we are, and this skews the relationship. In working with couples around critical upsets in their relationships, I tried to track the emotional process with each person, step by step. We looked at how each reacted to the other, and then what they decided to do around each reaction. The point was for each to know self better, to be more aware of self's part in the larger emotional process, and then to think about how self could be different at each juncture. The goal is to observe what is happening more objectively, and then to think about it (rather than just react) and make a thoughtful decision about how to respond.

Obviously this is not easy. It takes time and practice. But gradually we can train ourselves to behave differently in emotionally upsetting critical situations. It starts with knowing what we are doing and then setting a goal for how we want to do it. Then it takes practice in doing it. Personally, I am always surprised at the presence of my own anxiety and how it emerges. I am still learning about it today. Life usually gives us plenty of opportunities for practicing this learning.

At the end of *Persuasion*, Captain Wentworth discovers that he has wasted six years of possible happiness with Anne because, in his pride, he had failed to understand the nature of Anne's refusal to his first proposal of marriage. All those years he had blamed Lady Russell for persuading Anne to refuse him, and resentfully blamed Anne for succumbing to her persuasion. Now he sees it all more clearly, more objectively, as he talks with Anne. He sees his part, what he had totally missed. In chapter 23 he says to Anne:

"I trust to being in charity with [Lady Russell] soon. But I too have been thinking over the past, and a question has suggested itself, whether there may not have been one person more my enemy even than that lady? My own self. Tell me if, when I returned to England in the year eight [1808], with a few thousand pounds . . . if I had then written to you, would you have answered my letter? Would you, in short, have renewed the engagement then?"

"Would I!" was all her answer; but the accent was decisive enough.

"Good God!" he cried, "you would! It is not that I did not think of it, or desire it, as what could alone crown all my other success; but I was proud, too proud to ask again. I did not understand you. I shut my eyes, and would not understand you, or do you justice. This is a recollection which ought to make me forgive every one sooner than myself. Six years of separation and suffering might have been spared. It is a sort of pain, too, which is new to me."

In each of these cases, the person's worst enemy is self, not others. Their own lack of knowledge of themselves and how they function leads to misunderstanding both the other and the situation. But it takes a kind of moral toughness, courage, and maturity to face these truths about oneself. Some people live their whole lives without understanding this. Enlightenment about ourselves is often painful and even shaming. When we find ourselves justifying and defending our behavior with others, then we may be missing something important about ourselves. It requires character to be honest about ourselves. It is essential that we learn to get outside of ourselves in order to see what is going on in our relationships and how we participate in it all. It requires maturity to start this process, and it leads to greater maturity when it is achieved. Then we can develop greater responsibility for ourselves and we will be happier.

SEVEN

BEING RESPONSIBLE
FOR SELF

What are we responsible for?

Many things are beyond our control in life. No one is responsible for the circumstances they are born into, or for the many accidents of chance that life can bring to us. However, learning to take responsibility for ourselves, for the way we perceive situations, for the way we adapt and respond to them, for the decisions we make, and for the actions we take within these circumstances is more within our control. Taking appropriate responsibility is an essential aspect of developing emotional maturity. And responsibility for self is the basic presumption for developing goodness.

Being responsible for self includes being able to think and make judgments for ourselves. Early in *Northanger Abbey* we are told that the young and less mature Catherine Morland is not "in the habit of judging for her self." She has relied too much on the opinions of others and not done enough of her own thinking. She has some basically good instincts but she has not really thought much, for example, about issues of character. She knows that John Thorpe is not the best sort of person but she can't really say why or be specific about his shortcomings.

Thinking through issues in our relationships, and being able to sort out what part of the difficulty is ours and what is not, is critical to good relationships. Too often our focus is on the other person rather than on ourselves. This is frequently the case, for example, around the issues leading to divorce.

Divorce and responsibility

Thinking through whether or not to divorce a partner can feel just as difficult, if not more so, as deciding to get married. It is obviously a life-changing decision with many significant ramifications. Thinking through the issues involved and making the critical judgments that lead to divorce are major acts of responsibility in life. Often the partner who does not want a divorce, the one being left by the other, has not really thought all that much about the issues involved. They just know they don't want the divorce; they don't want to be left alone, or to break up the family. Circumstances are forced upon them that they do not feel responsible for and do not want.

Those who initiate a divorce rarely come in for therapy unless they want to find someone their partner can talk with after they leave. Usually those who don't want to divorce show up at my office after their partner has left. Such people come in two basic types. One group approaches therapy with a bitter, angry stance. They aren't sure that they want to change themselves and get on with their lives; they are really more interested in being angry with their former partner and blaming that person for their current unhappy experience.

> The critical first question to address after a divorce is "What was my part in the difficulties?"

This group, both men and women, believe they have been cheated, either around the facts leading to the divorce or in the divorce settlement, and this is only further evidence for them of the injustice and meanness of their partner. In therapy they focus on these issues or try to plot ways to get their former partner back.

Eventually, in working with such clients, when they could not respond to any other focus, I would wonder out loud if they thought they were ever going to get emotionally divorced from their partner or if they would be fighting with them to their grave. I told them I didn't care how they answered but that they would be wasting their time and money if they wanted to work with me just to keep building their case against their former partner and continue arguing the justice of their own cause. I couldn't help them.

Some of these clients then moved over to the second, larger group of divorcees—people who, while still feeling hurt, bitter, and resentful, were more willing to take responsibility for their lives and get on with living within these circumstances that they would not have chosen. This was not easy work, and I was often impressed with their strength and courage.

Part of their work consisted in figuring out what their own part was in the marriage coming apart. A few of these clients were much too willing to take nearly all of the responsibility for what happened in the marriage. These are the clients who said, "If only I had been more loving (or understanding, or forgiving, and so on), then this would not have happened." They usually accepted too much responsibility, believing that they were responsible for their partner's experience and behavior. I'm sure their partner, during the marriage, took advantage of this attitude as much as he or she could.

Most others, in this second group, faced the more difficult task of sorting out their own part in the marital dance. The critical first question to address after a divorce is "What was my part in the difficulties?" If people do not address this question, it is likely they will repeat the same problem behavior in their next relationship. We do repeat our patterns unless we consciously become aware of them and develop the means for changing them. My mother was married four times. Only late in her life, as she and I talked about it, was it clear to her that she had married essentially the same kind of guy each time (although outwardly very different), and the failures of these marriages had partly to do with her as the chooser, and then how she lived within the marriages. Of course, the men contributed plenty to the difficulties, but she had her part in them.

Two other questions are important for divorcees to address with respect to their marriage. First, once they recognized that there were difficulties in the marriage, what kept them behaving in the same old way? In other words, what kept them from attempting to make personal changes in the way they behaved? The attempt to answer this question usually revealed some underlying anxiety or fear within them, and a magical hope that things would just get better on their own.

A second question is "In a new relationship how will I recognize the repetition of old personal patterns of behavior, and what will I do about it?" Some understanding of the answers to these two questions allows people to enter into new relationships with more awareness, thoughtfulness, and confidence.

There is one other interesting issue related to divorce and responsibility in therapy. While very rare, it does happen that the "leavers" (the ones who initiate the divorce) come in for therapy saying, "I know I didn't do this right and I want to make some changes in how I live my life." Most of this group almost universally see the former partner as "the problem" in the marriage. And I think they are set up for more difficulty in later relationships than are the "leavees." The leavees, if they can get beyond their hurt, anger, and bitterness, have more of a chance to think about themselves and their part in the failed relationship. Consequently, they will do more growing after a divorce. For example, my mother was always the leaver in her marriages and she always thought it was the men who were the problem. Only late in her life did she focus on what in her own family experience had led her to choose the kind of men she did.

The will and being a victim

There is a concept in psychotherapy called "learned helplessness." It is a pattern that lies beneath much depression. The concept was developed by doing experiments with dogs that were restrained and then given unpleasant electric shocks. Since they were restrained, the dogs learned it was futile to try to escape the shocks. They simply lay there and accepted them. Later the restraints were removed, but the dogs did not try to run away from the shocks. They just continued to lie there whimpering, passively accepting the painful experience. They learned to be helpless in unhappy circumstances. We also can become so conditioned to painful experiences in which we believe we are helpless that we simply endure them rather than do something about them. We have no will to change our situation. Abused people can learn to be this way as well as depressed people.

We don't talk much about "the will" today, partly because we know that most of our personal difficulties cannot just be easily "willed" away. Change is hard work. The will consists of two parts: clarity of intention and discipline of behavior. Every dieter knows about this. It means consistently exercising choice over what we will and will not do at each juncture in what we choose to eat. Willpower, like any physical strength-building exercise, requires determination and a focus on the goal of how we want to be. It gets better and somewhat easier with practice.

At the beginning of *Sense and Sensibility*, Mrs. Dashwood and her daughters lose their home and most of their income when Mr. Dashwood dies a premature death. Their loss of home and income was due to the male-oriented inheritance laws in effect in Austen's day that gave all assets to the closest male relative, in this case to an older son from a previous marriage of Mr. Dashwood's. This is a major blow to the women's way of life and financial security. They, along with most women of their times, are truly victims of an unjust legal system. They then, in addition, have to endure the arrogant, hypocritical attitudes of their already-wealthy half brother, John Dashwood, and his wife, who take over their house and live-lihood. But this injustice and the insensitivity of privileged relatives are not an automatic blow to their ability to be grown-up, happy, and emo-tionally mature people. They are still responsible for themselves within these unhappy circumstances, which were not of their choosing.

All of Jane Austen's heroes experience some kind of significant loss in their lives, like the untimely death of a parent, or the loss of a childhood home or of family income. Life has dealt them more than their fair share of blows. Additionally, as women, they have practically no control over the circumstances of their lives. Emma is an uncommon exception as a hero for Austen. She does not need to marry for the sake of economic secu-rity. There are no male relatives who could steal away her inheritance. Of all the heroes, she has the most material advantages and the most ability to influence her environment and circumstance, and yet she is the least mature emotionally. As the famous opening sentence of the book says, so far things have pretty much gone her way:

We, like Jane Austen's heroes, often experience significant losses in our lives. We may lose loved ones through death or rejection; we may lose jobs, income, position, security, or opportunity; we may lose friendships through separation or betrayal. Often we bear some responsibility for the losses we experience. In such loss, when we become aware of and accept our responsibility, our character is strengthened.

Character and maturity—or the lack of character and maturity—come into play in shaping how we respond (or react) to the experience of loss.

- *Reflect on your own experiences of loss. How did you handle them? What did you learn from them?*

- *In what ways have your experiences of loss contributed to your emotional maturity?*

- *What connections have you noticed between the experience of loss and the exercise of willpower?*

Emma Woodhouse, handsome, clever, and rich, with a comfortable home and happy disposition, seemed to unite some of the
best blessings of existence; and had lived nearly twenty-one years in
the world with very little to distress or vex her.

However, her mother died while Emma was quite young. And both
her father and governess were too indulgent to be able to help shape her
character. Her story shows the common modern theme that one can be
both happily situated materially and immature personally. Someone has
said that real character emerges in people when they begin to be aware of
their mistakes and experience regret. This is the case for Emma. When
we first meet her she is rarely aware of making any mistakes or having
anything to regret.

The real evils, indeed, of Emma's situation were the power of
having rather too much her own way, and a disposition to think a
little too well of herself; these were the disadvantages which threatened alloy to her many enjoyments. The danger, however, was at
present so unperceived, that they did not by any means rank as mis-
fortunes with her.

Fanny Price, in *Mansfield Park*, is Emma's opposite, having nothing to
draw upon of a material nature to bolster her identity. All that she has is
her own person. We know that she is emotionally abused in her adopted
home at Mansfield Park, and there is a hint that her actual father also
physically abused her. She has some of the personality characteristics of
an abused child, including a tendency (unlike Emma) to think very little
of herself. She shows the most anxiety of any of Austen's heroes and she is
a less enjoyable person than they. Many readers do not like her (including
most of Austen's own family) because she is not bright and sparkling like
Elizabeth Bennet or Emma Woodhouse.

Fanny's early personal damage clearly slows her growth and development toward emotional maturity. She has a strong set of moral values but
she is not as emotionally mature as the other heroes in how she lives them
out. As a young person, first living in near poverty with her own disorganized family in Portsmouth, and then as a Cinderella type at Mansfield
Park, she has few external resources and little training to draw upon. She

could easily have had a career as an emotional victim, blaming others for her sad life. Austen shows us how she grows beyond the limitations of her history and manages, by the end of the story, to become the most mature influence within her adopted home of the Bertrams.

Fanny's personal history of abuse, misuse, and humiliation does not become an excuse for her. She does not see this history as automatically limiting her ability to manage her own moral life and her way of relating to others. She slowly develops and exercises greater willpower around being less of a wimp and becoming more the grown-up person she wants to be. She takes greater responsibility for her life rather than blaming her family for who she is.

Parenting and the responsibility for self

Ultimately, people are responsible for their own satisfaction and fulfillment in life, regardless of circumstances. Parents, however, play a part in the development of maturity in their children and their ability to be responsible for self. Parents can give their children a major boost in developing their own sense of responsibility. But this is a difficult challenge. It is easy to be confused about all of this and who is responsible for what in families. I call it the responsibility tangle.

> Parents teach responsibility for self primarily through example, by being responsible themselves; not by telling their children to "be responsible."

I have often seen parents try to "make" their children more responsible. In the process, just by virtue of doing this, they end up taking more responsibility for their children. A simple example is the parent who ends up virtually doing his or her children's homework. Or there are the parents who search the "Help Wanted" ads for their grown-up, unemployed child. Such parents are, often unwittingly, enablers of irresponsibility.

In *Pride and Prejudice*, after her daughter Lydia has run off with Wickham, Mrs. Bennet fails to see her own part in the situation, "blaming every body" but herself. As we read in chapter 47:

> Mrs. Bennet, to whose apartment they all repaired, after a few minutes conversation together, received them exactly as might be expected; with tears and lamentations of regret, invectives against

the villainous conduct of Wickham, and complaints of her own sufferings and ill usage; blaming every body but the person to whose ill-judging indulgence the errors of her daughter must be principally owing.

Parents teach responsibility for self primarily through example, by being responsible themselves; not by telling their children to "be responsible." By being open about their own mistakes, showing how they address them and take responsibility for them, and working out realistic remedies for their actions, parents show their children how to be grown-up people. If the parents tend to blame others for their own mistakes and unhappiness, like Mrs. Bennet does, then the children may do the same and not take responsibility for their own lives.

One client in her early thirties was having trouble coming to terms with her two marriages and with the kind of men she tended to get involved with. She was separated from her second husband because he turned out to have the same problems as her first husband. The husband was a drinker, abusive, and unfaithful. Her mother had resisted her first divorce, as well as this latest separation, saying, "Look, dear, this is just the way men are. Nothing can be done about it. They are just little puppy dogs who do what they want and rely on us to keep their lives going for them. Just scratch their tummies for them and they will be happy." My client saw how her life had turned out just like her mother's and she wanted to change the script she was living. She didn't want to teach her own children the same lessons.

So many parents make excuses for their children's bad behavior and don't let them experience the consequences of their actions. When I was much too young, I took on a newspaper route without telling my mother. The first day, while we were folding our papers, I was overwhelmed with fear when the older paperboys "pantsed" one of our number (i.e., took off his pants and threw them up in a tree). Then, after being the last to get my papers all folded, I discovered I couldn't ride my bicycle with the heavy paper bags hanging from my handlebars. The bags were swinging all over, causing me to frequently fall and dump all the papers. Adding to my troubles, I didn't know the route and where the streets were.

In frustration, I went and dumped all of the papers behind a building. That evening my boss started calling me with complaints from people who didn't get their papers. I swore that I had delivered them. Finally my mother intervened and made me tell what had happened. I felt truly ashamed, but that didn't get me off the hook. We then went and got the papers and delivered them all on a cold, snowy, dark night. I learned that responsibilities have to be fulfilled, and I never did this kind of thing again. My mother could have chosen to get angry with my boss and blame him for hiring me and providing so little guidance and support. But she didn't work that way.

As a family therapist, I often saw parents talk about responsibility to their children. That is not unusual. But their own lack of clarity about responsibility in relationships led them to act in either irresponsible or over-responsible ways themselves. They were often not good at taking responsibility just for themselves. For example, it is not uncommon for parents to say to a child, "You are driving me crazy," and then use the child's behavior as an excuse for engaging in unhelpful or damaging behavior of their own. They fail to demonstrate the kind of behavior they want from their children. Instead, they communicate to their children that they are responsible for their parents' feelings and behavior.

Parents can get emotionally focused on and over-involved with either their "favorite" child or the one in whom they have, for a variety of reasons, the greatest emotional investment in his or her doing well or succeeding. Often this is also their most difficult child. In any case, the self of the parent gets wrapped up in the self of the child and it becomes difficult to sort out the tangle of responsibility. Consequently, the child learns to see others as in charge of self. It is only one further step for the child, when in trouble, to say to the parent, "You made me this way."

Lydia Bennet (*Pride and Prejudice*), Marianne Dashwood (*Sense and Sensibility*), Emma Woodhouse (*Emma*), and Maria Bertram (*Mansfield Park*) are good examples of this reality. All of them have greater difficulty in becoming mature and emotionally separate people because of the child-focused indulgence and confusion of their parents. The parents have sought good feelings about themselves from these children. Mrs. Bennet, for example, almost relives her life through her daughter, Lydia. This warps Lydia's sense of self and her responsibility for self. Mrs. Norris, who is a kind of substitute parent (due to Lady Bertram's abdication of the role), significantly indulges Maria's behavior and enjoys sharing her life with her. This leads to a major tragedy for both of them.

Getting untangled responsibly

Growing up is a gradual process of parents letting go of responsibility for their children, and children assuming more of it. This is a difficult transition, as any parent or young adult knows. Had I been older, my mother would not have interrupted her life to help me deliver the papers; she just would have insisted that I do it. And if I were older still, she wouldn't have thought about it at all. It wouldn't have been her job any longer.

Becoming a good and mature person requires this gradual assumption of responsibility for self. However, this process becomes difficult when the parent is confused about who is responsible for what. Parents have to have a clear sense of the emotional separateness between themselves and their children. Things like feeling sorry for a child, or not wanting the child to feel hurt, or always wanting the child to be happy with them as parents, can get in the way of this clarity.

Mature parents have a sense of the importance of emotional autonomy in relation to the circumstances of life. Immature parents tend either to see others as in charge or, conversely, to believe that they are fully in charge of others—like their children. The opposite of emotional autonomy is emotional fusion, which involves confusion about who is responsible for what. In the emotional responsibility tangles of family life, parents are not always sure where they stop and start emotionally in relation to their children, or a partner, or whoever. As a result, the children will also tend to be confused and be less responsible for self.

My mother had to wonder what to do about my not having delivered the papers. Probably her first sense of responsibility was to the customers, so she took responsibility for what I had not done. She must have realized that, at my age, I was not up to dealing with the paper delivery job. In the process, I learned clearly how I had failed my responsibility. She told me the next morning that I must call my boss, apologize, and say that I would not be coming back. Most readers can probably remember times when they have learned similar lessons.

Child-focused parents often have a sense that their parents did not do enough for them or were not adequate in some way. I have seen many parents who wanted to provide for their children what they believe they did not get from their own parents. They think their parents were inadequate (which might have been the case) and they will make up for this with their children. This rarely works but it becomes a goal in their parenting. They make their children their project in life. This usually results in their taking too much responsibility for the children and not enough responsibility for their own lives. The children will have difficulty becoming mature, grown-up, and responsible adults.

Most of Austen's heroes rise above the level of emotional maturity of their parents primarily because they, unlike the more problematic young women above, are not their parents' favorites. Because they are on the outside of the intense relationship with the more favored siblings, they are freer to develop more independently of the parents.

Anne Elliot (*Persuasion*) and Fanny Price (*Mansfield Park*) are two heroes who are in "outside" positions in their families. They were not the favorite children of their parents. This leads to their suffering a certain amount of emotional abuse and neglect, but ultimately this is not damaging to them. Their outside position gives them perspective, an ability to think about what they observe and to decide more easily how they want to live their lives. Favorite children get focused on, and get much more caught up in, their parents' ways of thinking and feeling. Being outside of this intense family emotional process allows less favored children to be more objective; they can be freer spirits as a result.

> Over-functioning parents take responsibility for things in their children's lives that are not their responsibility.

The favorite children, or the ones more focused on, usually do less well in life and love, partly because they become dependent on being the emotional focus. Consequently, they are not clear about how to simply be in charge of their own life and happiness. A child who is not the favorite or more focused-on sibling is better able to develop a self, as long as resentment about not being the favorite does not become an issue. One oldest daughter client finally got over her resentment of "all of the love and attention" her younger sister got from their mother when she realized how debilitating this was for her sister. Her sister was never able to establish an independent life of her own. The older sister decided she was happy to have been a freer spirit, not caught up in so much emotionality with her mother.

Taking responsibility for self is pretty much a natural development for children when their normal development is not interfered with. Over-functioning parents take responsibility for things in their children's lives that are not their responsibility. This tends to produce under-functioning children who take less responsibility for their lives and well-being. Seeing the children under-function, the anxious over-functioning parents become even more involved in trying to make things happen for their children, thus producing children who are even less responsible and more under-functioning. It is a truly vicious cycle.

People who were under-functioning children will often become partners in marriage who expect much to be done for them. They will be high maintenance, either physically or emotionally. They typically marry someone who will over-function for them. These people (both partners), in spite of appearances, will not be people of good, strong character because they are focused on the other providing for them rather than on the self's own responsibility.

The over-functioning partner (often thought of as "the good one") participates in this irresponsible behavior. Both partners are involved in the confusion of who is responsible for what. In therapy I usually had more luck coaching over-functioning people in reducing their level of responsibility for others. Under-functioning people tend not to raise their level of functioning until there is no one left who will function for them.

One set of parents referred their adult son to me after his marriage had come apart within the first year. His wife found him irresponsible and lazy and she wanted nothing more to do with him. He was devastated and moved back home with his parents. His parents had heard me give a public lecture on over- and under-functioning in relationships, and they knew they both had over-functioned for their son. They were a little unhappy that I insisted on seeing them with their son, but they soon got the point. They thought that I was somehow going to make their son more responsible. They hadn't really gotten the point of the lecture even though they recognized the problem.

They still had their own work to do in relation to him because the old patterns at home were getting started again. Being highly motivated, they quickly got much clearer about the responsibility tangle and began to sort out what they would and wouldn't do for him in his present circumstances. In response, he became even less responsible, tempting them to take charge again. But they became quite good at taking charge only of their own behavior and he eventually got the point that they would not again become responsible for him or simply allow him to live with them forever.

Marianne Dashwood (*Sense and Sensibility*), a favorite of her mother's, finally recognizes that Willoughby has jilted her. After she nearly dies from her deep, emotionally based physical reactions to his abandonment, she could easily have focused on his bad behavior as the source and cause of her unhappiness. But while sick, she learns to think more clearly about her own responsibility for her sadness; she rises above her mother's own tendencies to see others as responsible for her emotional condition, and she lays the blame for her disastrous reactions directly at her own feet. In chapter 46 she says to her sister Elinor:

> Do not, my dearest Elinor, let your kindness defend what I know your judgment must censure. My illness has made me think. It has given me leisure and calmness for serious recollection. . . . I considered the past: I saw in my own behaviour, since the beginning of our acquaintance with [Willoughby] last autumn, nothing but a series of imprudence towards myself, and want of kindness to others. I saw that my own feelings had prepared my sufferings, and that my want of fortitude under them had almost led me to the grave. My illness, I well knew, had been entirely brought on by myself by such negligence of my own health, as I had felt, even at the time, to be wrong. Had I died, it would have been self-destruction. I did not know my danger till the danger was removed.

In her usual style, Marianne is being somewhat dramatic as she expresses a significant realization. But she is taking more responsibility for her life and no longer blaming either her feelings or her illness on Willoughby or anyone else. She acknowledges within this confession that she has been rude, uncaring, selfish, unkind, and contemptuous of both friends and family. But she does not say it was because of her own victimization, or blame it on Willoughby's bad behavior or her parents' failure to guide. She says, "My own feelings had prepared my sufferings."

Being responsible for self puts us in touch with the power to change.

Of course, others do behave in ways that either enhance or detract from our happiness, depending on our wants. We can change our wants, just as Marianne lets go of wanting Willoughby and learns to love Colonel

Brandon. If she continued to insist that Willoughby was the "one and only" man for her, she might then have died of depression, spiritually if not physically. Rather than passively remaining caught up in her loss of Willoughby, Marianne eventually takes more control of her life. Being responsible for self puts us in touch with the power to change.

❦ Eight ❧

Having a
Goal-Focus in Life

Other-focus and being a victim

We hear a lot in the media today about people's angry behavior toward others. I don't know if it is true that we live in an angrier time than any other age. I do believe we are an increasingly less civil society and more likely to vent our rage publicly when we are frustrated. This rage is generally caused by a sense of being victimized in some way by others. We know of "road rage," "air rage," "school rage," "computer rage," "postal worker rage," and many other such violent displays. Each can be deadly for the person affected as well as for others. While the majority of us are not so extreme, we can still be abrupt and discourteous to others when we think they have negatively affected us in some way. Many people have justified their rudeness to others as "just being authentic," and they believe they have a right to behave this way if others have not done right by them.

Rage and the ensuing lack of civility go along with the sense of being victims. You may have read about a man who shot and killed three of his neighbors because they set off fireworks near his home. He felt like a victim and he was going to "pay them back" for disturbing his peace. Clearly he is a disturbed man and his anxiety, in the form of rage, took over his behavior. He seems to be no longer all that rare. Last year I was driving a friend's car on a highway in California, driving at the stated speed limit. Another driver pulled off a side road in front of me, moving at a slow pace. After braking hard, and somewhat angry, I honked the horn to make sure he was aware of me. My California friend said, in a serious tone, "Careful, that guy might have a gun." He said he thought about this possibility every time he drove his car.

> Mature people do not focus on the symptoms or difficulties that result from the actions of others.

Many of us have lost the will to focus on developing personal strengths and character in the face of difficulty and unhappy circumstances. Rage is one symptom of our lack of character. We display the symptoms of being victims and dwell on our supposed problems so much that we end up nurturing them. More mature people do not focus on the symptoms or difficulties that result from the actions of others. Their own direction in life transcends the problems they encounter. They aim to be the best person they can be within the circumstances they are given.

Part of what makes Austen's heroes so attractive is that they refuse to think of themselves as victims. They are often treated badly by others and do not receive the respect they deserve. While they can be as anxious about life and relationships as we may be and have similar difficulties, they focus on developing their personal strengths, rather than being defeated by their limitations or by the opposition of others. They are not focused on their problems or difficulties.

Even whole cultures can take on a victim identity. When a people focus simply on their often very real oppression and victimization, they usually stay stuck and stagnant. They don't grow and move ahead. They get caught up in issues of blame and retaliation. People who focus on their goals will have a more positive identity. For many centuries, Ireland dwelt on its victimization by England, and much of the country remained poor and dispirited. By contrast, the new, modern Ireland is an example of what can happen when there is a focus on what a people want to become rather than on how they have been held back.

Many of the couples I saw in my practice blamed each other for their own unhappiness, or for being stuck in their lives. Or they may have regarded one or both of their parents as the source of their difficulties, saying, in essence, "It's their fault I am not the person I would like to be." As a result, they displayed the symptoms of unhappy people. People often become their symptoms. It is their identity and their focus in life.

One person attending a conference on relationships asked the speaker a question that I heard often in my practice: "Why should I be loving toward my partner when she doesn't act loving toward me?" The speaker quietly responded, "Because you need the practice." This is the difference between an "other-focus" and a focus on becoming a better self.

For our own good and the good of our relationships, it is important that we interrupt the automatic reactive cycle of responding to attack with attack in order to get even, and to stop feeling done in by these attacks.

Relationship conflicts are opportunities for us to become better people, to be the way we want our partner to be with us. Focusing on what we think is the other person's problem and how that is a problem for us keeps us reactive to them. Focusing on how we would like to be with them, regardless of how they are with us, helps us to move along toward a better life and probably, but not always, a better relationship.

We never hear Jane Austen's heroes say something like, "You make me so angry," or "You hurt me," or "You made me do it," or "You ruined my life," blaming others for their unhappiness. They regard their happiness as up to them and not simply the result of more felicitous circumstances. Research has shown that people who are often angry at others for some real or perceived damaging behavior very often end up getting more hurt emotionally or even physically ill. The damage and hurt just keep building.

Goal-focus versus other-focus

Personal goal-focus, as opposed to other-focus, is about the goals we set for ourselves; it is about how we want to be with other people, as well as where we want to head in life generally. Goal-focus is an essential ingredient of good relationships. Other-focus is about how we want others to be with us. It is more about how we think others impact our interests and how it is their job to make us happy. Or possibly, in the reverse, how it is our job to make others happy. This makes for very difficult and confusing relationships.

In doing marital therapy, I often asked a partner, "What would you say is the most difficult thing about living with you? What kind of a challenge do you represent for your partner?" It is surprising how many people thought these were novel questions and had never thought about them before. They could tell me a great deal about their partner's problems and how difficult he or she was to live with, but very little about how they were difficult for their partner. My question got them thinking about how their own behavior contributed to and interconnected with their partner's difficult behavior. Honestly looking at and addressing these questions took courage. Those who were able to do so began to think about and set goals for their own behavior and paid less attention to the other-focused attempt to change their partner's behavior.

One woman began a session telling me how her husband had angrily thrown a volleyball at her and hit her on the side of her head. She then berated him in the session while he sat there quietly. I interrupted her and said, "Wow, you must have really got to him. How did you do that?" She first looked at me puzzled, and then she said, "Well, he and our son were playing with the volleyball in the yard, and I came out to sit awhile in the sun. I asked him to not take up so much of the yard with their game. He said they were there first. Then I snapped and said to him, 'You selfish SOB, you don't have to take over the whole yard for your stupid game.' And he blew up and threw it at me." This led to her bursting into angry tears and to him, feeling justified, berating her for interrupting him while playing with their son, "which is something you always say you want me to do." They said this was typical of their kind of arguments.

I didn't mean to suggest, with my question to her, that she was responsible for his being violent with the volleyball. That is never the case. She didn't "make him" throw the ball at her. No one "makes" another person violent. She didn't even "make" him angry, and he didn't "make" her speak as she did. But each believed and acted as if the other was responsible for their own behavior. Since she was presenting herself as the innocent victim, I wanted to make clear that there was an emotional process they both participated in and that either one could have interrupted their own part in this devolving interaction. But in fact, they each acted as if the other was in charge of self, and being the victim of the other, they struck out in rage; he physically and she verbally. In their reactions, they were each focused on how they wanted the other person to be rather than on how the self could be.

By personal goal-focus, I am not talking about being self-centered or selfish. Self-centered people are generally unreliable friends, inattentive family members, and irresponsible in whatever positions of authority they hold, whether as workers, parents, employers, or heads of families. Mrs. Norris (*Mansfield Park*) is able to be efficient and well organized, and she clearly has goals, but they are self-centered. This leads to poor judgment for her, time after time. She is able to maintain her position as female head of the household by flattering Sir Thomas and over-functioning in relation to his wishes and responsibilities. But this is simply to keep the boss on her side so she can do what she wants; she does not really care about his concerns.

Toward the end of the novel, when Tom Bertram, the eldest son, has become deathly sick and Maria has abandoned her husband and run off with Henry Crawford, Mrs. Norris is left alone with Tom and his under-functioning, incompetent mother, Lady Bertram, who is her sister. Her own usually over-functioning style transforms into a deeply depressed under-functioning. Her carefully constructed world is falling apart. It is a very unhappy household. In chapter 47 each of them is focused on her or his own misery.

> [Mrs. Norris] was an altered creature, quieted, stupefied, indifferent to everything that passed. The being left with her sister and nephew, and all the house under her care, had been an advantage entirely thrown away; she had been unable to direct or dictate, or even fancy herself useful. When really touched by affliction, her active powers had been all benumbed; and neither Lady Bertram nor Tom had received from her the smallest support or attempt at support. She had done no more for them than they had done for each other. They had been all solitary, helpless, and forlorn alike; and now the arrival of the others only established her superiority in wretchedness. Her companions were relieved [when Edmund and Fanny returned], but there was no good for *her*. Edmund was almost as welcome to his brother as Fanny to her aunt; but Mrs. Norris, instead of having comfort from either, was but the more irritated by the sight of the person whom, in the blindness of her anger, she could have charged as the daemon of the piece. Had Fanny accepted Mr. Crawford this could not have happened.

The family, individual behavior, and goal-focus

There are no under-functioners without over-functioners. Other people play a part in the development of these "problem" people. They go with each other like hand and glove. Whenever I saw clients whom most people would consider a "problem" person who needed help, I automatically wondered who, in the course of their lives, had tried to "help" them. If these people were available, I invited them into therapy as well. They often came with the sense that they would "help" me help the problem person. Gradually they began to see, however, that they were a part of the problem. I rarely saw under-functioners raise their level of functioning until their "helpers" backed off from their over-functioning, until no one else was taking responsibility for their anxiety.

We cannot simply finger the over-functioners like Mrs. Norris or the under-functioners like Lady Bertram as "the bad guys" in a family. Their behavior is interconnected with that of others. Sir Thomas's and Lady Bertram's behavior allows Mrs. Norris to behave as she does. In this sense, they are irresponsible. They are all equally involved. The difficulties and problems of the family lie within the way each person in the family functions, not simply in individual people. This is the nature of family emotional systems.

Starting early in life, under-functioners have had someone who over-functioned for them, who took responsibility for what they actually could have done for themselves. All babies, obviously, are under-functioners. Gradually, in the process of growing up, they learn to do for self as the parents stop doing for them. If, however, the parents continue to "wipe the child's nose whenever it runs," then the growing young person may continue to rely on the parents to meet his or her needs into adulthood. Over-functioners often believe that other people's happiness or success is their responsibility or that they have to give up self and live for others to get love and acceptance.

When my mother made me go get the newspapers I had dumped and she, borrowing a friend's car, took me around to deliver them, she was over-functioning for my under-functioning. Although her doing so was appropriate at that point in my life, it would have been a problem if she had made excuses for me and continued this kind of behavior as I aged, because I would not have learned to take responsibility for myself. I got the point of her lesson that night. It was my job to do what I said I would do. It was not her job.

> Over-functioners often believe that other people's happiness or success is their responsibility or that they have to give up self and live for others to get love and acceptance.

Neither over-functioners nor under-functioners are "the bad guys." This is not a matter of blame. They have just built their sense of self on the presence and actions of the other. This is part of our other-focus. This is a normal human process, part of the responsibility tangle. Most over-functioners think their behavior is a good and caring way to be. Most families function with this emotional mechanism to some extent. It is a part of what is called emotional fusion. The self of one person is fused with that of another. The more mature the family is, the less there is of this over/under-functioning process, or the less fused they are. Each person can function as a more emotionally autonomous or independent self, responsible for self's functioning.

We are all dependent on one another in some form. That is the nature of a cooperative society or a family. We are interdependent. We help each other out in difficult circumstances. People are not left to flounder helplessly when they are in trouble. We provide whatever support we can to one another. This is normal helpfulness. But when we consistently do for others what they could do for themselves, then we are not actually helping. We are contributing to their debilitation, to an inappropriate dependency, through this over/under-functioning reciprocity.

Change comes about in such a symptomatic family system when at least one person (hopefully the over-functioner) starts taking more responsibility for self and gets self emotionally untangled from the under-functioners while still actively relating to them. This person makes a project of changing self rather than the other. This is what I mean by getting emotionally untangled, by becoming less fused.

Goal-focus is about this personal, self-focused effort. When we are successful at being different from how we have functioned, others in the system are then challenged to be different themselves. Under-functioners are challenged to change when others stop taking responsibility for them. But this focus on self is not done for that reason. If it is, it won't be successful. Such behavior is still a kind of other-focused over-functioning.

Goals and principles

Our goals for the kind of person we want to be in life are based on our chosen principles and values. We need to clarify our beliefs about what is important to maintain and uphold and what we will affirm and live for in our actions. The focus of this work is not so much on "What will other people say?" or "What do they want me to be?" or "How do I get them to do my bidding?" but on "What do I believe and value in how I live my life?" and "What do I think are my responsibilities?" and "How do I want to be?" Personal goal-focus is difficult to maintain on a consistent basis. We would rather focus on others and how they can make us happy by doing what we want or disappoint us by refusing to do so.

Fanny Price, the hero in *Mansfield Park*, is an excellent example of maintaining a principled, personal goal-focus even in unhappy circumstances. In the passage below, Austen calls it her "sternness of purpose." Some of

Fanny's goals are to be considerate, helpful, caring, and responsive to the needs of others, even to those who have treated her badly. She believes this is important for her in order to be a responsible member of the household she has been adopted into. Her cooperativeness, however, is misunderstood by the family. As a matter of principle, she is not an easy pushover for what others want her to be. She can, at times, firmly stand her ground even when they put a huge amount of pressure on her to be the way they want and to, in essence, cooperate with them in their irresponsible behavior. She will not act against her principles just so others will be happy with her.

Fanny's problem is communicating her position to others, because she is still somewhat other-focused in this area. She is so anxious not to upset or hurt anyone with what she thinks they might regard as harsh words or an ungrateful stance that she cannot easily communicate the reasons for her position. Probably her experience with her own explosive father affects this. She is too anxiously careful and out of touch with this part of herself. She does not want to be courted by Henry Crawford, but she can't clearly and firmly tell him this. Her inability to be fully in charge of herself contributes to others not being clear about where she stands. In this area she under-functions. In chapter 33, Austen says of her:

> Fanny knew her own meaning, but was no judge of her own manner. Her manner was incurably gentle; and she was not aware how much it concealed the sternness of her purpose. Her diffidence, gratitude, and softness made every expression of indifference seem almost an effort of self-denial; seem, at least, to be giving nearly as much pain to herself as to him.

Flattery and self-assessment

One of the most consistent examples in Austen of other-focus is revealed in flattery. Flattery is different from giving a compliment. Flattery is when we are trying to get something from others, like approval or acceptance. A compliment has no agenda other than to show appreciation. For example, a man who is giving a line to a woman he is trying to pick up may use flattery. If she responds positively, he is probably going to achieve his aim. She may even say to him, "Flattery will get you everywhere."

Both the flatterer and the one depending on flattery are other-focused. Flatterers need to win over the object of their flattery to get the self-centered rewards they seek. But the one receiving the flattery also participates in the emotional process. A man who responds to a seductive woman's comment, some version of "You are so big and strong," has a need to hear this about himself, especially from a beautiful woman. His sense of self is dependent on getting that. Other-focused people need to have others think well of them in order to feel good about self. All of us can enjoy a compliment, but when we "need" these to survive emotionally then we may well be in difficulty.

Just one of many examples of flattery in Austen is the wonderful scene in *Pride and Prejudice* in which the Collins party, including Elizabeth, is invited to dinner at Lady Catherine De Bourgh's estate house. Rev. (Mr.) Collins cannot resist again ingratiating himself to the wealthy Lady Catherine. Vain people need the admiration of their admirers and the admirers need the approving smiles of the object of their praise in order to feel okay. In chapter 29, Elizabeth wonders at how such fawning could be comfortable for Lady Catherine, but then sees that she delights in it.

> Other-focused people need to have others think well of them in order to feel good about self.

The dinner was exceedingly handsome, and there were all the servants, and all the articles of plate which Mr. Collins had promised; and, as he had likewise foretold, he took his seat at the bottom of the table, by her ladyship's desire, and looked as if he felt that life could furnish nothing greater. He carved, and ate, and praised with delighted alacrity; and every dish was commended, first by him, and then by Sir William, who was now enough recovered to echo whatever his son in law said, in a manner which Elizabeth wondered Lady Catherine could bear. But Lady Catherine seemed gratified by their excessive admiration, and gave most gracious smiles, especially when any dish on the table proved a novelty to them.

The young Catherine Morland, in chapter 7 of *Northanger Abbey*, did not know how to resist the oafish efforts at charm of John Thorpe at the Bath assemblies. Catherine was naive and inexperienced in courtship, and she fell, unwillingly, for Thorpe's flattery.

Had she been older or vainer, such attacks [of flattery] might have done little; but, where youth and diffidence are united, it requires uncommon steadiness of reason to resist the attraction of being called the most charming girl in the world, and of being so very early engaged as a partner.

"Steadiness of reason" gives us the ability to do self-assessment, a basic requirement for goal-focus. Emotional dependency means we build a self on the basis of what others want, expect, and appreciate, rather than on what makes sense to us. Many a partner in a troubled marriage has complained to me, "I don't know what happened. When we first started dating, he (or she) made me feel so good about myself. But now it's like he (or she) hates me. I feel terrible." When our sense of self is dependent on the flattery of others, we are then vulnerable to their change of affections and their moods.

In chapter 8 of *Northanger Abbey*, contrast Catherine's susceptibility to flattery, and her friend Miss Thorpe's need for it, with the more mature demeanor and presence of the attractive Miss Tilney, who is at the same ball with Catherine. Clearly young women today can behave in the same way they did in Austen's time.

> Miss Tilney had a good figure, a pretty face, and a very agreeable countenance; and her air, though it had not all the decided pretension, the resolute stylishness of Miss Thorpe's, had more real elegance. Her manners showed good sense and good breeding; they were neither shy nor affectedly open; and she seemed capable of being young, attractive, and at a ball without wanting to fix the attention of every man near her, and without exaggerated feelings of ecstatic delight or inconceivable vexation on every little trifling occurrence.

This passage is such a wonderful description of what all young (and many older) women struggle with. It is an excellent example of what emotional maturity looks like in the romantic setting of a dance. In matters of love, courtship, and even friendship, we ought not to substitute others' flattery, or their lack of attention to us, for our own reasoned self-evaluation. When others comment on us, either positively or negatively, we then have to see if that checks out with our own self-assessment.

The very attractive Mary Crawford, in *Mansfield Park*, is a woman of the world who appears competent and comfortable in life, but Austen says that Mary has "a prevailing desire of recommending herself." This means she wants to "look good" in the eyes of others, rather than "be good" in her own eyes. She needs the attention of others. When others are not around to admire and entertain her, she becomes bored. She cannot stand to be alone and not have someone's attention focused on her.

Being goal-focused does not mean we ignore feedback from others. The comments and reactions of other people are some of the ways we learn about ourselves. Elizabeth and Darcy provided feedback to each other even in their anger. Eventually they were both able to hear the angry statements of the other and think about what parts of them were true. They did not ignore the comments because they were said in anger. They were able to use the comments in doing their own self-assessment.

We should not, however, substitute others' feedback for our own reasoned self-evaluation. When others comment on our behavior and words, then we have to see if that checks out with our own self-assessment. Of course, this can be difficult and requires a high degree of objectivity. When people say things about us that we do not like, we must carefully consider whether they have picked up on something in us that we have been blind to. What was our part in the negative reaction of others? We may be as

Jane Austen's novels demonstrate the danger to self of flattery. Both the one who flatters and the one who welcomes being flattered are other-focused people. The flatterer needs to win over the object of his or her flattery in the service of selfish needs. Personal integrity is the victim. The one flattered loses a sense of true self by building a false self on the basis of the exaggerated (and self-serving) "compliments" of others. Again, personal integrity is the victim.

- *In what ways might wanting to look good in the eyes of others lead to behavior that makes it more difficult to be good in your own eyes?*

- *Reflect on the saying, "There is no worse slavery than slavery to the opinions of others." How might such slavery cause people to compromise their values?*

- *How might honest, careful self-assessment liberate one from such slavery?*

much to blame as the other person. As difficult as it is, mature people will do this self-assessment more readily and seek to change their negative behavior if any is found.

Setting personal goals and connecting with others

In her novels, Jane Austen's larger social world is peopled with those who are rude, vain, greedy, unprincipled, and foolish. There are also kind, thoughtful, caring people of good sense. Her heroes manage to relate to all of these people in a civil way without losing their own integrity. Their challenges are the same as ours. The Christian virtue of "loving our neighbors as ourselves" is a basic principle for having a more civilized society. It does not mean loving only those who are like us and who share our values or approach to life.

Moving toward our personal goals creates satisfaction and happiness in life and makes for better relationships. Less mature people, in their focus on others, either try to compliantly become what others want or try to change others to be what they want. This sets them up for either continuous dissatisfaction—since others will never be what they want—or false and empty relationships in that people cannot truly be themselves when they are being compliant with the wants of others.

Lady Catherine De Bourgh, in *Pride and Prejudice*, is a wonderful example of someone with a strong desire to change others to fit with her wishes. She rarely looks to changing herself. Her mood and happiness are totally dependent on whether others are doing what she wants. She wants to be in charge of all of those around her. Only those who depend on her, like her eating-disordered daughter, or those who wish to flatter her, like Rev. Collins, do what she wants. Lady Catherine cannot have a real friend. She cannot have a genuine emotional connection with others. She has a selfish focus, not a self-focus.

Elizabeth Bennet can see Lady Catherine's foolishness. Even so, she behaves in a civil, polite, and as friendly a way as she can with her, and is an appreciative guest in her house. She does not need to "honestly" tell Lady Catherine what she thinks of her. She is tactful in her relations with her. Only later, when Lady Catherine barges into the Bennet household and rudely demands that Elizabeth not marry Darcy, calling her all sorts of names and saying that mixing the Bennet family with hers and Darcy's will "pollute" them, does Elizabeth become more honestly straightforward and say more of what she thinks. Still, she mostly stays focused on defining herself. When pushed, she voices the principle that when it comes to her own happiness, she will not take into consideration the concerns of someone like Lady Catherine—someone who is "so wholly unconnected with me."

Emotionally mature people are caring and compassionate people.

However, at the end of the novel, in chapter 61, we see Elizabeth doing her best to reconcile with Lady Catherine. She wants to reestablish the connection. Rather than react to Lady Catherine's continuing rudeness with anger, she focuses on her own goal to define herself in a friendly way toward Lady Catherine, and to include her as part of the family. She encourages Darcy to do the same.

> Lady Catherine was extremely indignant on the marriage of her nephew; and as she gave way to all the genuine frankness of her character in her reply to the letter which announced its arrangement, she sent him language so very abusive, especially of Elizabeth, that for some time all intercourse was at an end. But at length, by Elizabeth's persuasion, he was prevailed on to overlook the offence, and seek a reconciliation; and, after a little farther resistance on the part of his aunt, her resentment gave way, either to her affection for him, or her curiosity to see how his wife conducted herself; and she condescended to wait on them at Pemberley, in spite of that pollution which its woods had received, not merely from the presence of such a mistress, but the visits of her uncle and aunt from the city.

Austen's mature goal-focused heroes do not become socially isolated from those around them. Self-focus does not lead to emotional isolation. In affirming their mature individuality, in being strong and solid people, they do not abandon or lose social connection. At the end of their stories, her heroes end up being better connected with family and friends and more respected. In fact, they often emerge as leaders within their community.

Emotionally mature people are caring and compassionate people. This is normally one of the outcomes of mature, goal-focused individuality. They can be attentive to the needs of others without being solicitous or ingratiating. As family members, they are responsive to the upsets that others experience and freely offer to be of help. As friends, they are good listeners and provide reliable support, doing what they can when a friend is in difficulty. Because of their own principles and values, more mature individuals have a more secure emotional connection with others, are capable of caring behavior toward them, and are able to work together cooperatively for common goals.

Nine

Feeling and Thinking

Feeling and thinking as guides to living

Years ago I heard a famous movie star interviewed about her decision to get married. She said, "It just feels right. I am responding to my heart. That's how I work. You know, whatever feels right at the time." I remember wondering how well the marriage would work if this is how she makes decisions. Two years later I heard that she was getting divorced. She said, "It's no longer working. It just doesn't feel right anymore." I wondered if the decision to divorce wasn't as ill-founded as the decision to marry.

Feelings change according to the circumstances. When we are run by our feelings, we go up and down emotionally in reaction to the events of our lives. We are at the mercy of those events. We depend wholly on certain people liking us, or being loved by a particular person, or having things just the way we want them in order to feel good. Other people and circumstances set the emotional tone of our lives. And firm commitments get broken simply because they no longer "feel right."

It is easy to be run by our feelings. All of us do it and often it doesn't get us into big trouble. Often when things "feel right," they are. All this means is that the circumstances or the people around us harmonize with our wants and expectations. Things are going our way. This is what "right" means at the feeling level. All of us like it when this is the case; we usually say at these times that we are "feeling good."

Nevertheless, we need to be able to get some distance from our feelings at critical times because feelings tend to be too narrowly focused, often on the wrong thing. Normally I would help couples in my practice gain some distance from the anger, hurt, fear, and anxiety they experienced with one another. These feelings usually arose from their reactions to each other, their perceptions of the other, or the circumstances of their lives, but the feelings didn't really help them to better define themselves within their challenging relationships and circumstances. All they could do was react, react, react.

A critical factor in developing our emotional maturity is the ability to think more objectively about our lives within our web of emotional relationships. It is said that we put more thought into buying a car than we do into choosing a life partner. Of course, we can buy cars out of emotionality as well. I know of a man who bought a Ferrari (mostly because he could) and only then discovered that he couldn't get it over the hump at the entrance to his garage from the street because it was so low to the ground. He also didn't know how to drive it very well.

In most challenging situations, decisions about how we act have to be based on our best thinking at the time; not just on "what feels right." To do this, we need to know the difference between thinking and feeling and when we are operating out of one or the other. And we need to have the ability to choose which one we will be guided by at any particular moment. The more we are consistently guided by feelings alone, those in ourselves and in others, the less mature we are likely to be.

> Feelings can change when we develop a new interpretation of what is going on.

I am not saying that feelings are bad. Our feelings are essential to being human. They give us a sense of vitality, a sense of involvement, connection with others and with life, a passion both for things we care about and for things we oppose, a sensitivity to others that allows us to better empathize, the ability to care for others who are in difficulty or pain, and the ability to participate in the joy of others as well. Feelings are an essential part of the spirit of being alive.

Feeling and subjectivity

Feelings also reveal our inner emotional state in response, usually, to the external circumstances and relationships of our lives. They give us information about ourselves within those circumstances. Feelings are inevitably subjective. That is, they make us the subject of whatever happens. In this sense, feelings are necessarily self-centered. They put us at the center of the story, even when the story isn't really about us. Our feelings tell us about our perception of our position in relation to others. When we hear about other people's tragedies and feel bad, it is because we can put ourselves into their situation and imagine something of what it is like. This is empathy. Most of us, when we hear about the execution of a vicious serial killer, don't "feel bad" about the tragedy of his execution. We don't put ourselves in his situation.

Feelings can change, even within the same circumstances. Feelings are a combination of our basic emotionality, something we have in common with all human beings, and our own unique individual interpretations of what is going on in our lives. This is why different people in the same situation "feel" different. Feelings can change when we develop a new interpretation of what is going on. Out walking on the street, a man steps on my toe and walks on by with barely a sideways glance. Naturally outraged (basic emotionality) and angry, I chase after him and say, "Hey, why don't you look where you're going?" Only then do I realize he is blind. My feeling of anger changes drastically due to a new interpretation of the situation. My toe still hurts because it was stepped on, but I have given the pain a new meaning. All of our feelings are subject to this kind of personal interpretation of the circumstances. This is why they are subjective.

For example, one quite complicated feeling in love relationships is jealousy. Some of us are more affected by this than others, and it may vary from one relationship to another. Certainly it has to do with our personal sense of threat (basic emotionality), along with what the possible loss of a person who is important to us means to us. How we assess our own level of threat and how we interpret the situation are contributing factors to jealousy. Jealousy is often called "the green-eyed monster," partly because when it takes over, we generally lose contact with objectivity. We don't see the true color of things, and it runs our lives in a single-minded way. We narrowly focus on just the immediate situation.

Thoughtful, intelligent people can totally lose their ability to think when they become jealous, and most often they act in ways that undercut their goal of keeping their partner. Wishing to better secure the relationship with our loved one, we will often drive him or her further away from us through our jealous actions. We lose the ability to be balanced, weigh the facts, and accurately assess reality.

A few of my clients have found themselves alone simply because of their overpowering jealousy. One man observed his wife having fun with a single man at a party. Before this event, because of some accurate observations on his part, he had suspected a secret relationship was going on between this man and another woman. Nevertheless, watching his wife have fun with this man, he lost sight of that observation and his jealousy took control of his thinking and feeling. He became highly critical of the man and attacked his wife for having anything to do with him. Jealousy took over and colored his every interaction with both of them—and he nearly lost his wife. Only when the relationship between the man and the other woman came out into the open did he get over it, and like his wife, he ended up rather liking the man.

Subjectivity skews our perception away from what is most likely true and changes it into an issue of whether something or someone is a personal enemy or a friend, whether there is a threat to us or not. Remember, anxiety results from the experience of threat, real or imagined. Then we add our personal subjective interpretation of what is going on, which is often out of touch with all of the facts, and we end up acting in unhelpful ways. Once the client was clear that the other man was not after his wife, and that his wife had no romantic interest in the man, he could get back on an even keel.

Like us, Austen's characters grow and become more mature whenever they can more objectively see the bigger picture and when they can push their reactive feelings aside and stop making the story be just about them. Even Anne Elliot (*Persuasion*) and Elizabeth Bennet (*Pride and Prejudice*), two of Austen's most mature and thoughtful heroes, have to struggle with misreading Wentworth's and Darcy's signals. They tend to interpret the men's words and actions as being negatively about themselves, when they are really just about the men's personal characteristics and history. But Anne and Elizabeth both "take it personally." This is subjectivity. This lack of objectivity leads them to misunderstand what is going on at a personal cost.

Many of the couples I worked with struggled with this. They took the character traits of their partners personally. As a result of their subjectivity, how their partner saw life and the world and functioned within it, including in relationships, determined whether they felt loved.

Here is an example. Driving to their therapy appointment, a man said to his wife, "Aren't those flowering trees beautiful?" She said, "Yeah, I guess, if you like trees." When they came into the office still fighting over her response, she insisted that her statement was simply factual. She said she never takes much notice of trees. He took it personally that she "never" seemed to like what he liked. It was important to him, subjectively, that she share his likes and dislikes. This example may seem petty, but it was a big deal for the man involved because, he said, "it is so typical of her."

Because Elinor Dashwood (*Sense and Sensibility*) is able to achieve a degree of objective detachment in the midst of her emotional turmoil when she discovers that Edward, the man she loves, is secretly engaged to Lucy, she has a good outcome in a very difficult set of relationships. She is able to get more outside of herself. She is not run by the jealousy she could easily feel. To her great credit, she is even able to think (and feel) sympathetically about Edward and what it must be like for him to be engaged to Lucy. Thus she is able to maintain perspective in her difficult encounters with both Lucy and Edward. Had she simply reacted with her subjectively hurt feelings, the whole situation would have been more difficult and she would also have been more miserable. She might even have lost Edward.

Feelings are an inadequate guide to living. Back in the 1960s and '70s, a number of us adopted the phrase, "If it feels good, do it." That simple little phrase got many people into big trouble. Many marriages came apart during those years primarily due to the affairs people had that "felt good" at the time. Personal friends of mine went through some difficult years and later regretted choices that had been guided by their feelings. They now say, looking back, that they made some really bad choices. Their problem was not that they had feelings, but that they put their feelings in charge of their lives.

One client was "bored" with her life with her husband. She had been a housewife and a mother of two school-age children. Then she had an affair with "a very exciting man" and life was "wonderful" for her. She ended up leaving her husband and became "the bad guy" in the eyes of her kids. The two lived together briefly, and then the man ("the love of my life") moved on to another relationship. She hadn't heard the saying that when a mistress moves in with her lover, she immediately creates an opening.

She didn't want to try to get back with her husband and he was too angry with her to consider it. A bitter divorce resulted. When she came in to see me, she was totally bereft and struggled to makes sense of it all. In therapy she did a lot of hard thinking. As a result of the divorce settlement, she was able to go to graduate school and eventually got a good job, but relationships with men continued to be a challenge for her, primarily because of issues of trust and the kind of men she was still drawn to.

The first two years of therapy were tumultuous because of her feelings. Gradually she began thinking more clearly and staying more goal-focused. I began to have appointments with her once a month. She was not significantly involved with any man during this period and she began to accept the idea that "that might never happen." She said, "Looking back, that affair was one of the dumbest decisions of my life. I had these romantic feelings and they were wonderful at the time, but I just wasn't thinking. I could have had all the good things I have now, have a better relationship with my husband and kids, and not been so lonely if I just hadn't acted on those feelings." It was sad. She was doing a good job of putting her life back together and living as an independent woman, but it was truly a bittersweet success.

Elinor and Marianne Dashwood (*Sense and Sensibility*) are sometimes characterized as being, respectively, the personification of a thinking-dominated person (sense) and a feeling-dominated person (sensibility). But Austen is not that simplistic. These two characteristics exist in both of them, as they do within all of us. Marianne is clearly able to think and Elinor is clearly able to feel. In fact, Austen describes Elinor as a person of "strong feelings." However, Marianne's thinking is often more subjectively based on her feelings. Her feelings guide her thinking. In important situations, they do not help her to see reality more objectively. And this is what gets her in trouble.

One place where it is very clear that Elinor and Marianne have different ways of dealing with their feelings is when both Edward and Willoughby have left the Dashwood sisters and gone away (chapter 19). Marianne, the romantic, fulfills her role to the fullest, so that everyone knows she is bereft of the love of her life. Elinor, however, resolves to show no such loss to anyone since Edward has made no declaration (quite correctly as it turns out) of his love for her. In reality, neither had Willoughby for Marianne, but she acts as if he has because of her strong desire that it be so. Elinor wills not to make an overt expression of her feelings. Marianne knows of Elinor's loss at Edward's departure although she does not know the whole story. She is horrified at Elinor's unwillingness to express her feelings around this loss.

Austen makes clear that there is a distinction between having feelings and deciding when or whether to express them. It is not that Elinor is against the idea of expressing or sharing her feelings. It is not even that she is overly reserved, as Marianne would charge. Partly, she does not want to open up her feelings with people who cannot handle them as she would wish. Her mother and Marianne would dwell on the feelings and become agitated and angry with Edward, thereby heightening her own sense of loss. It is easier for her not to talk about her feelings with them. She knows they would not try to think through the situation with her. If she had a friend who would do this with her, she would likely be willing to share with her.

Feeling and thinking are not opposites so that we always have to choose one over the other. They are two kinds of personal resources we have for making sense out of our lives and trying to figure out the best course to take at particular junctures. As with my client above, the feeling of being "bored" in marriage is useful information to have. The feeling tells us we might want to do something about our lives. But what to do, at that point, is something that needs to be thought about within the context of the big picture, our values, and our goals in life. We can all have trouble figuring out which direction to take at such junctures. First we have to understand the issues involved. And then we have to have a basis for making good decisions about our direction. We ignore our ability to think at our own peril.

In matters involving romantic love, it is particularly important to be able to think. Thinking is not a substitute for the wonderful feelings of attraction, but nothing can cause temporary insanity and rational dis-

Jane Austen's novels demonstrate that while feelings are normal—and we all have them—they are not an adequate guide for living, for making the choices that determine how we will (and will not) act in relationships.

Lest we be blinded by the subjective nature of our feelings, we need to develop the objective detachment that gives us space to think about what we feel, why we feel it, and what an appropriate self-focused (not selfish) response would be.

- *Make a list of the feelings you commonly experience and the kinds of situations within which these feelings arise.*

- *To what degree do the feelings take over and control your thoughts and behavior?*

- *To what degree does your thinking take over and enable you to respond in ways that express your principles of living in spite of your feelings?*

connect like romantic love. This is what happened with my client. She saw the romance as a solution to her boredom. Maybe we wouldn't fall in love at all without the intensity of feeling that accompanies it. It provides the momentum and incentive needed for the work that our relationships require. But it is really much better to "have our wits about us" in the midst of the experience than to just unthinkingly "go with the flow."

Expectations and feelings

Nearly all of the couples I have worked with in therapy ran into difficulty because they had differing expectations as to what marriage would be like, as well as differing expectations as to what their partner would be like and would provide for them in marriage. They did not get what they expected. When reality clashes with our expectations of how we believe things "should" be, or how our partner "should" be, we can become anxious, angry, fearful, or depressed. Then we try to get our partner to do what we want. If our partner doesn't, we may then "check out" of the relationship emotionally, if not physically, and perhaps seek satisfaction in life elsewhere. We may say, "The relationship is no longer working."

Much of marital therapy consists of looking at each partner's expectations and how they came to be important. Often our expectations go back to our own family of origin experience. Stated simply, we may be determined to have either exactly what we experienced in our family or exactly the opposite of what we experienced there. Usually our expectations are emotionally based, coming out of family experience, and it is that emotional experience that has made them so very important. The client mentioned above got into her affair partly because she had "suddenly realized my life was becoming boring just like my mother's." This terrified her because she had seen her mother live a subservient, somewhat depressed life, giving up a sense of joy and any aspirations for herself. Unfortunately, she saw her husband as the cause of her boredom.

> People who have relatively happy relationships over many years will tell you that part of what they each had to do was adjust their expectations.

One younger couple came in to see me after they had separated. She had initiated the separation and said that it was because they were fighting a lot. How, she wondered, if they really loved each other, could they be fighting so much? I asked how she got that idea and she said her parents had "a perfect marriage" and that they never fought. This was what she wanted for herself.

After a few more sessions, I suggested that she make a trip home and ask each of her parents how they managed to "never fight." She said, "Okay." When she got back from the trip, she was truly amazed. She said that both of her parents told her they "fought all of the time, still do after thirty years of marriage." Typical for their generation, they had agreed to "never fight in front of the kids." They didn't want to upset them. By doing this, however, the parents not only skewed their children's view of marriage; they robbed them of being able to see how they worked through their conflicts.

It takes a lot of time to sort out for ourselves what we think marriage or a particular love relationship will do for us. Why do we want to be married or have this specific relationship? What makes it important to us for it to be this particular way? Where does the emotional force for what we want come from? Is our desire realistic?

People who have relatively happy relationships over many years will tell you that part of what they each had to do was adjust their expectations. They may call it "compromise." When their expectations were not met, they looked at them and tried to decide what made them important emotionally and whether it was reasonable to hang on to them. Then they had to decide whether or not to insist on their expectations being fulfilled before they could find satisfaction in the relationship. Living with another person, or even maintaining a friendship, involves a lot of this kind of thinking.

We all need to have our "bottom lines" in a relationship, consisting of what differences between our partner and ourselves we will and will not accept. These bottom lines are based on our principles, beliefs, and values. A common one is "I will not tolerate my partner having an affair. If that happens I will leave." Generally we do not compromise on these. But so many things that we think are essential may, in fact, be open to negotiation. We can live happily without many of our expectations being fulfilled if there are other rewarding parts to the relationship. Our bottom lines, however, must not be used to constantly bludgeon and threaten our partner into doing what we want: "Do this or I am leaving."

Elinor's and Marianne's expectations of both marriage and their partners were quite different. Elinor had put more thought into these issues. Her expectations were pretty realistic, unlike those of the more romantic Marianne, and as a consequence, she was not so much a victim of her feelings. By the end of *Sense and Sensibility*, however (chapter 50), Marianne makes some major shifts in her expectations of marriage, the kind of partner she wants, and the kind of life she will have, and is consequently a much happier person.

> Instead of falling a sacrifice to an irresistible passion, as once she had fondly flattered herself with expecting, instead of remaining even for ever with her mother, and finding her only pleasures in retirement and study, as afterwards in her more calm and sober judgment she had determined on, she found herself at nineteen submitting to new attachments, entering on new duties, placed in a new home, a wife, the mistress of a family, and the patroness of a village.

Principles as the antidote to a feeling-based life

It is easy to believe that our feelings are the same as outward reality; that they are fact based. For example, one woman found a number of men she dated "scary," when her friends did not. She was sure that what she felt about them was real and had trouble separating her subjective feelings, about many things, from objective reality. It is a fact that we feel. That is real. But what we feel is not necessarily factual. The feelings may be accurate and useful, or not. We can accurately "intuit" some things that we can't explain logically. I always encourage clients to pay attention to their fears of other people, but this woman's feelings often misled her. Our feelings can mislead us about other people because the perceptions are very narrowly focused, based on our expectations and on how we personally are affected.

One wealthy divorced man I worked with was fearful and suspicious of most women. His marriage and divorce had been an unhappy experience for him partly because of these feelings. He thought his feelings were reasonable and fact based. He perceived women he dated to be "selfish gold diggers" and, as a result, could never establish a solid relationship with them. Talking this over with male friends, he knew "something" must be wrong with him but he couldn't get beyond these feelings. We took a long time to work at sorting out these somewhat paranoid feelings about women and he eventually became a "more realistic" person. He was able to address some of his "real" childhood experiences, and even talk with some of the people involved (which was very helpful for him), and figured out how these had affected his perceptions of relationships with women. He discovered that his subjective perceptions were most often not true.

Toward the end of the therapy, I told him that one well-known family therapist had said, "If you are not paranoid, you're crazy." He was able to laugh at the paradox and get its essential meaning, and said that he thought he had now escaped that dilemma. Although it was hard work for him, he began thinking about relationships in a new way. He began to find satisfaction in being close to a woman he was dating.

One of the things we did in therapy was to work out some realistic principles he could live by. One was the virtue of "generosity." Originally this virtue did not mean being willing to give of one's money (a big issue for him) so much as starting off a relationship thinking well of people and giving them respect, thinking they were doing the best they could do in life. To be a "generous person" in Austen's time meant to ascribe esteem to others; to think well of them until they demonstrated in their behavior that they were not worthy of this. I gave him this quote from Shakespeare's *Hamlet*: "Use every man after his desert, and who shall escape whipping? Use them after your own honor and dignity. The less they deserve, the more merit it is in your bounty." Of course, he found all of this to be a rather amazing idea, but he was willing to play with it

> Feelings come to us easily. Clear, objective thinking is a skill we have to learn.

and found it helpful. He began to ascribe good intentions to the people he met, women in particular, and he started complimenting them. He found he was getting a much different response from them, and it "felt" good.

Austen believed that the development of solid principles is a better guide for living our lives than basing our lives only on our feeling reactions. It takes self-examination and wisdom to understand our feelings and put them in perspective. Feelings come to us easily. Clear, objective thinking is a skill we have to learn. It helps if we are part of a family in which other members, like our parents, can often do this. Watching them engage in more objective thinking as they encounter the problems of life gives us a leg up on doing it for ourselves. If we grew up in a more emotionally reactive, less thoughtful family, it is much more difficult to do, but not impossible.

The naval officer Captain Benwick in *Persuasion* (chapter 11) is a person who needs some better, more thoughtful, principled guidance. His fiancée died while he was away at sea and he has never recovered from the loss. He dwells on it daily. Clearly a sensitive man, he reads melancholic poetry, something that only takes him deeper into his own sad feelings of loss. Anne Elliot sees this as the "nourishment of grief" and undertakes to advise him on other things he can read. His life is absorbed in feeling, and Anne attempts to show him the usefulness of principles. In his case it is the principle of fortitude she is attempting to inspire.

> He was evidently a young man of considerable taste in reading, though principally in poetry; and besides the persuasion of having given him at least an evening's indulgence in the discussion of subjects, which his usual companions had probably no concern in, she had the hope of being of real use to him in some suggestions as to the duty and benefit of struggling against affliction, which had naturally grown out of their conversation. . . . He showed himself so intimately acquainted with all the tenderest songs of the one poet, and all the impassioned descriptions of hopeless agony of the other; he repeated, with such tremulous feeling, the various lines which imaged a broken heart, or a mind destroyed by wretchedness, and looked so entirely as if he meant to be understood, that she ventured to hope he did not always read only poetry, and to say, that she thought it was the misfortune of poetry to be seldom safely enjoyed by those who enjoyed it completely; and that the strong feelings which alone could estimate it truly were the very feelings which ought to taste it but sparingly.

One client had lost her husband in a tragic car accident while he was on a trip overseas. She was so distraught that she could not deal with the arrangements of bringing his body home, and her eighteen-year-old son had to do this. Many months later she was still so focused on her loss that she just wasn't able, as her friends advised her, to "move on." In fact, she hated it when anyone said those words to her. She did not want to "move on." It seemed to her that to do so would be to deny the happiness of what she had had and to accept the "injustice" of what she had now. It was so very difficult to get outside of the subjectivity of her grief, and the fact that her life had been drastically changed by "a ridiculous accident," that she just refused to "accept it." She had so many ways of nourishing her grief that she neglected what needed to be done now.

When we only "go with our feelings," we often make poor decisions that are neither in our own best interest nor considerate of those around us. Her son was so upset about how his mother was affected that he wasn't able to focus on his own grief and loss of his father. She didn't see this at all. She just relied on him to do things for her and to keep her life running while she continued to grieve. She was not generally a selfish woman; she just couldn't see the reality of what was happening. Only gradually over a period of time, as we talked about the kind of values she wanted to maintain in her life and how well she was doing that, did she get more objective and less dominated by her feelings of loss.

It was a similar situation with both Marianne and Mrs. Dashwood (*Sense and Sensibility*) over the occupation of their home by the new owners. Again, Elinor is able to get outside of her own subjective, angry reactions. While she could agree that the John Dashwoods unnecessarily rushed their assumption of being masters of Norland Park estate, she knows that to angrily focus on this unchangeable fact and to behave resentfully toward them will only make matters worse. She considers it neither honorable nor generous to behave uncivilly toward them simply because of their lack of sensitivity and crude assumption of their legal rights. In chapter 1, she chooses principle (sense) over reactive feelings (sensibility), in comparison to her sister and mother.

> Elinor saw, with concern, the excess of her sister's sensibility; but by Mrs. Dashwood it was valued and cherished. They encouraged each other now in the violence of their affliction. The agony of grief which overpowered them at first was voluntarily renewed, was sought for, was created again and again. They gave themselves up wholly to their sorrow, seeking increase of wretchedness in every reflection that could afford it, and resolved against ever admitting consolation in future. Elinor, too, was deeply afflicted; but still she could struggle, she could exert herself. She could consult with her brother, could receive her sister-in-law on her arrival, and treat her with proper attention; and could strive to rouse her mother to similar exertion, and encourage her to similar forbearance.

Elinor's feelings are strong; she is "deeply afflicted," but she knows how to "govern" them. Anne Elliot (*Persuasion*) also has to struggle mightily with her feelings whenever she encounters Captain Wentworth. Thinking that he can no longer be interested in her romantically, she has to find ways to quell the beatings of her own heart. The use of reason is the primary resource she has for managing her own unreturned feelings of love and attraction to Wentworth. As we read in chapter 7:

> Soon, however, she began to reason with herself, and try to be feeling less. Eight years, almost eight years had passed, since all had been given up. How absurd to be resuming the agitation which such an interval had banished into distance and indistinctness! What might not eight years do? Events of every description, changes, alienations, removals—all, all must be comprised in it, and oblivion of the past—how natural, how certain too! It included nearly a third part of her own life.

Of course, Anne is not successful in stopping her feelings for Captain Wentworth. But she is able to get enough control over herself so that she does not make a fool of herself and act on ideas that, as yet, have no basis in fact.

Thinking through our feelings

Much of my therapy with people consisted in asking questions that evoked more "thoughtful" responses. I helped people get some emotional distance from their immediate experience. I rarely asked the typical therapist question, "How does that make you feel?" Most of my clients, when they felt safe enough, expressed their feelings spontaneously without any prompting from me. In fact, wives were often surprised when this happened because

| We need to think about our feelings.

they had thought of their husbands as "unfeeling." However, being able to *reflect* on feelings, on our lives and circumstances, rather than just reactively feeling, is more of a challenge. It is essential to having a better life and good relationships. We have to be able to more objectively reflect on who we are and how we function in our relationships. This thoughtfulness helps us to exercise better judgment.

As we grow and mature, we develop greater skills in making good judgments. This is an essential part of the virtue of prudence, or what we now call wisdom. Wisdom is more than having knowledge. It may start

with knowledge, but then we have to exercise judgment and learn to dis-
criminate between what may be true or false, "smart" or "foolish." Most of
our foolishness is lack of wisdom, which stems from a lack of good judgment. We all struggle with this.

We need to think about our feelings. We are not always clear about
what we feel. Sometimes we feel "mixed up." We may have lots of feelings about a person or a situation and not know what to make of them.
Elizabeth Bennet (*Pride and Prejudice*) spends a lot of time trying to figure out what she feels in relation to Mr. Darcy. In this case "feelings" represent not only her conscious, subjective emotional experience, but also
her behavioral stance or attitude toward the man. Will she incline herself
toward or away from him? Will she be warm or cool? Will she be friendly
and open or only civil and polite, if that much?

Much of the book records her up-and-down feelings about Darcy.
Throughout she has to struggle to think clearly, moving from subjective
reactions to more objective thoughts. She has to get over her feelings of
"pride" in being able to judge character (incorrectly as it turns out) and her
"prejudice" against Darcy as a rich, rude snob. She struggles to be a wiser
judge of people. Austen doesn't tell us much about Darcy's struggles, but it
is clear that he has had his own struggles with pride and prejudice and has
had to learn to be more thoughtful and wiser.

Later in the story, while visiting his Pemberley estate, Elizabeth begins
to see the real Darcy more clearly. She sees him in a wider context, separate from her reactions to him. She now perceives that he is a good and
benevolent landlord, a kind employer, a warm and caring brother, and even
a polite gentleman. She knows that her attitude has changed significantly
from hate to . . . what? In chapter 44 she lies awake trying to figure this
out.

> As for Elizabeth, her thoughts were at Pemberley this evening
> more than the last; and the evening, though as it passed it seemed
> long, was not long enough to determine her feelings towards *one*
> in that mansion; and she lay awake two whole hours endeavour-
> ing to make them out. She certainly did not hate him. No; hatred
> had vanished long ago, and she had almost as long been ashamed
> of ever feeling a dislike against him that could be so called. The
> respect created by the conviction of his valuable qualities, though
> at first unwillingly admitted, had for some time ceased to be repug-

nant to her feelings; and it was now heightened into somewhat of a friendlier nature by the testimony so highly in his favour, and bringing forward his disposition in so amiable a light, which yesterday had produced. But above all, above respect and esteem, there was a motive within her of good will which could not be overlooked. It was gratitude. —Gratitude, not merely for having once loved her, but for loving her still well enough to forgive all the petulance and acrimony of her manner in rejecting him, and all the unjust accusations accompanying her rejection.

This is a case where rationality and feelings work together. She knows she feels differently now when she is around Darcy. With greater objectivity, her interpretations of him have begun to change. She no longer thinks of him as she did. Her confusion and change of attitude keep her from allowing, just yet, that she may in fact love him. She knows she is stirred up emotionally. It keeps her awake for "two whole hours." If she were Marianne Dashwood, she would not have slept at all. She tries to think through his behavior and his warmer stance toward her and her present response to it. She compares her actual behavior to her professed principles. Elizabeth is getting clearer about her own behavior, seeing it in a larger context.

Austen's heroes are able to think about their feelings, to make a distinction between what is feeling based and what is based on objective fact and behavior. They attempt to discern what is true for other people, not just for themselves, and how others impinge on them emotionally and, equally important, vice versa. They use the ability to be more objective and thoughtful about their experiences as their primary resource in solving the problems of life. This more objective thinking helps the heroes to be clearer in developing their own character and principles as well as in improving their relationships.

❧ TEN ❧

CHARACTER AND PRINCIPLE

A principle-based life

Emotionally mature people live principle-based lives. Character is built on principles and it provides the ability to live according to those principles. The more maturity we have, the more we will be able to live by the principles we profess to believe in, especially in difficult and challenging circumstances. However, rather than acting from principle, our natural inclination when we are anxious or feeling threatened is to act on our feelings of the moment out of the short-term self-interest of reducing our anxiety. Being able to delay gratification of immediate desires, pursuing our long-term goals, and living by self-chosen principles is the way to a satisfying life.

It's true; virtue is its own reward. The long-term Harvard Study of Adult Development has followed a large group of Harvard graduates since the 1940s. Of course, if they are still alive, they are now quite old. Those who are considered to have been generally "good people" have lived the longest, had the best health, and have been characterized by the researchers as "giving, generous, and kind." There is a great deal of other contemporary research data saying the same thing.

More than any other time in history, we are bombarded with media images of people behaving in less-than-virtuous ways. "Winning" at all costs, by whatever means, is becoming the standard for different types of leaders. So-called reality TV shows are a prime example of this kind of ethic. Whatever the field, be it politics, athletics, the business world, music and the arts, or even religion, many of our leaders are failing to lead as moral examples.

Our principles are fundamental assumptions about what we believe to be important and true about living our lives and relating to others.

They may espouse values and good principles for living, but often they are discovered not to be living by them personally. They say one thing and do another. And we may find ourselves becoming more cynical as a result.

Our principles are fundamental assumptions about what we believe to be important and true about living our lives and relating to others. They are general truths basic to how we make decisions in our everyday life. For example, the principle of self-government affects our beliefs and practices with regard to democracy. It helps us decide things like what is fair or not around electing our representatives in government. Principles provide direction for us at specific points in our lives, in specific circumstances. They do not tell us exactly what to do in those circumstances, but they provide criteria to use as we try to think about, evaluate, and make judgments about how to act.

Character and "being real"

Good character is one of the primary terms that Jane Austen uses for what I am calling emotional maturity. She shows us people who are able to live up to their principles in emotionally difficult circumstances. There are many principles and virtues shared by all of Austen's heroes. Civility, for example, is one. Many of us have become less civil, even with those we love. Being honorable is another. Generosity, in the sense of attributing good to others, is the other side of this. It is ascribing honor to others. Another is constancy. Today we call it commitment. It is the ability to remain faithful to what we have promised to do, rather than being turned aside by "better opportunities" or other temptations.

> To be authentic is to be in charge of our story, or of the development of our self, as we write our own story with our lives.

We have lost sight of traditional principles like civility and constancy because they do not fit with what has become a popular psychological stance called being "authentic" or being our "real" selves. This stance grants permission to act on the feelings of the moment because that is considered "authentic." This approach says, "This is your real self and you are just being honest." Marianne Dashwood's romantic philosophy would fit in well with contemporary culture.

Following the more complacent, post-war Eisenhower years, the 1960s gave birth to several new ways of living one's life. One of the offshoots of the hippy movement was devoted to "sex, drugs, and rock and roll." Honesty was supposed to be a primary virtue of the hippy lifestyle. They said whatever they thought. They "let it all hang out." After telling someone "like it is," they said, "I'm just being honest, man."

There were some positive benefits to this way of living, but many of the people who actively pursued that lifestyle ended up wasting their lives. Some died young because of drugs. They did not build the new society they imagined partly because their principles were inadequate for the communal life they espoused. Honesty was not balanced with other important principles, like kindness and civility. Their "authentic" incivility was destructive of the community life and good relationships they wanted to create. The same can be said about many other types of movements, including religious ones. All too often, such movements are intent on achieving some cause by focusing on just a few narrow principles, rather than on simply being good.

The word *authentic* comes from the same Greek root as the word *author*. To be authentic is to be in charge of our story, or of the development of our self, as we write our own story with our lives. We define our principles and goals as a part of this self-development. Today some people refer to this as "agency." We are the active agents of our own lives, rather than being passively acted upon. As agents we decide what principles we will live by and how they will be lived out in specific situations.

Choosing to act according to one's principles rather than one's feelings is not a denial of authenticity. Feelings change with the circumstances, but principles can remain firm through all sorts of situations. Indeed, when we just go with our feelings, there is no true, consistent, authentic self within us to affirm. To be a solid and authentic person is to be faithful to what we believe in and want to be. The authentic person has a more solid character.

Developing character in our emotional environment

Austen agrees with modern family systems therapists that the emotional context of our family and social environment plays a major part in shaping who we are. However, she would not agree with the belief of a few therapists that people are simply the impotent victims of their families and social environment. I agree with her that we have a greater ability to become masters over our lives and to change the direction of our lives, through a courageous act of will and intentional decision making, as we continue to relate to the important people in our lives.

Today we often look at a person's behavior within a psychological context rather than through the lens of character. Some of us have come to believe, for example, that we have an emotional right to respect. We are then upset and angry when we don't get it. Some therapists even suggest that our not receiving the love and respect we "deserve" is what causes us to behave badly as adults. This idea is actually ethically regressive. Of course, everyone deserves respect, but our not receiving it does not justify our own disrespectful behavior. The idea of excusing our adult behavior because of our unmet emotional needs as a child, or lack of respect as an adult, has led us to ignore our personal responsibility for the development of good character. It boils down to blaming others for who we are and our way of thinking and living.

There is no question that many, if not most, of us experienced some kind of emotional deficit in the parenting we received as children. Some of us experienced more than a deficit—it was outright damage. There are no perfect parents. Our parents are people just like us, maybe worse, maybe better, who have had their own challenges in life and made plenty of mistakes. But a focus on what is due from them, or from others, has made achieving a satisfying, contented life nearly impossible for people who think this way. The other-focused orientation of wanting our "emotional rights" respected by others has taken precedence over principles like self-control, responsibility for self, and respect for others. These contemporary values lead only to more and more self-centered and narcissistic people who have great difficulty being in relationships because they are so sensitive to the possibility that their feelings are not being respected.

Many of my clients, male and female, came into therapy complaining of a lack of respect from emotionally important others. This is indeed a modern complaint, one we have learned from our culture. Going in a different direction, I asked them, at some point, about how *they* respected themselves and what this would consist of. How did they get it? Did respect from others necessarily precede self-respect? What would this self-respect imply about how they acted toward others? The principle of respect for others is too important to hold up our own growth until we get it from others. Being respectful is more important in good relationships than waiting to get it.

Fanny Price was born into a poor, significantly disorganized, disrespectful household in Portsmouth, a rough southern port city. At the age of ten she is invited to move to a wealthy aunt's household. She comes to the Bertram household as a fearful, uncertain wimp. She is most comfortable hiding in a corner somewhere and not interacting with anyone in the household, where she continues to experience a significant amount of disrespect. Edmund, the second Bertram son, befriends her and mentors her. She does not expect respect from others, but he shows it to her, most of the time.

The story of *Mansfield Park* is about how Fanny grows up and becomes a mature person of character who can handle herself confidently with anyone in the household, while also being a kind, considerate, helpful, and caring person. Her growth does not depend on getting respect from others. It happens in spite of their disrespect. She is respectful of others and eventually she gains respect from them. Finally getting their respect had

Fanny Price, the hero of Mansfield Park, *is a good example of how character is formed by focusing on one's own behavior rather than on the behavior of others and the feelings that behavior elicits.*

Practicing self-chosen virtues such as kindness, generosity, civility, and commitment, regardless of how others respond or react to you, leads to emotional maturity and the freedom to "author" your own life.

- *In what ways does culture in general and the media in particular encourage if not promote unvirtuous behavior?*

- *What resources are available to you that encourage and promote virtuous behavior?*

- *Reflect on how you do (or don't) author your own life.*

- *What virtues tell the story of your life?*

WE ARE ALL STORIES.
THE QUESTION IS: WHO IS THE AUTHOR? ME OR "THEM"?

to feel good to her, but it was not her goal. Her goal was to be good. That was more important than getting respect.

Developing character is about moving beyond our personal hurts and damaging experiences and becoming the person we wish to be rather than a person simply determined by and reacting to those hurtful actions of others. Fanny consistently demonstrates a determination to be in charge of her life and behavior in spite of the attempts at humiliation and the abuse she suffers. The abuse does not become an excuse for her behaving badly. Fanny could have become a basket case if she had focused on all the wrongs done to her. Today, she might be in therapy for many years.

I once had a client, Hildy, whose parents had been servants in a wealthy household in South Africa. As their child, she was taught to stay out of the way, do what she was told, and be quiet unless spoken to. Her childhood was not a happy one. She happened to have married a wealthy man after she immigrated to Canada. She was generally a person of good character. But she behaved in her marriage much the way she did as a child in the wealthy household where she was the child of servants. She did what was expected of her by her husband. But she was emotionally unavailable to her husband and children, socially reclusive, and somewhat depressed. Like Fanny, who felt most herself when she was in her own "East Room," Hildy lived much of her life within a private world that she told no one about.

Her one area of outward rebellion, however, was that she generally took the side of her adolescent children whenever they rebelled against the wishes of their father. This was her way of fighting with him by "supporting" them. They were her surrogate rebels. In therapy she was very slow to look at her own life and goals. It was difficult for her to define how she wanted to live her life. She also had to separate herself emotionally from her children and decide to let them work out their own relationships with their father. There were some tumultuous times in this family because the children refused to relate to their father like she did. But slowly she began to see herself more clearly, in the context of what her life had been, and set out to become a different person.

Eventually we invited her husband, whom I had met at the beginning of therapy, to come in with her. He testified to the changes he had seen in her. He said he didn't like all of them—like when she openly disagreed with him—but that he felt he had more of a real partner and that he respected her more. I saw her children also and they said much the same thing. Hildy slowly became a more open, assertive, real, mature self and became more socially active as well. Claiming the competencies she had, she began taking leadership in community events. Hildy reminded me of Fanny Price. The point is, however, that none of these changes could have been given to her by others—such as her often patriarchal husband. She had to claim them for herself. As she did, he also began to change and eventually came in for therapy for his own issues.

Having a strong, more solid self does not mean becoming uncivil. For example, we can both be assertive and have good manners. The insistence of some therapists on the full, open, and truthful expression of all feelings means that manners often take a backseat in our relationships today. It is ironic that we tend to be most unmannerly with those we are closest to, our partners and other family members. For example, Austen's heroes show respect for their parents even when they are behaving like silly fools. This does not mean they always do what the parents want them to do. Elizabeth Bennet will not marry Rev. Collins no matter how much her mother demands it. But at no point does she "honestly" tell her mother how foolish she is for wanting this.

Today we tend to be suspicious of well-mannered people. We think they may be hypocrites because we know they are not saying all that they think or feel. Austen also knows that bad character can hide behind good manners. Most of her bad characters are people who are capable of being well mannered and charming. She knows that manners are a surface phenomenon that, to be genuine, have to be supported by an underlying, principled goodness.

Another positive sign of a good character is the ability to control one's emotional reactivity—what Austen calls "temper." We do sometimes still speak of people being in a "bad temper" or losing their temper. The ability to control one's temper is the strength that keeps us from inappropriately saying or automatically showing what we are feeling. Austen's heroes are able to moderate their tempers and contain their automatic emotional reactions when someone behaves badly toward them. They can choose when and how they will express these feelings, if at all.

One couple came in for marital therapy after the wife discovered that her husband was having an affair. This is a frequent enough occurrence for therapists, but in this case, the husband was a clergyman. He was charming, well liked by his congregation, and generally a polite, well-mannered, and temperate man. But he became infatuated with a woman living in his small town (not a church member) and said, "I just could not help myself." This affair was not known to his congregation.

Early in therapy he terminated the affair. I saw the husband and wife separately and together. They each had reactions to the immediate situation that were best discussed separately. When they were each ready to focus on rebuilding the marriage, we began a two-pronged approach that involved first looking at how they were each functioning in their marriage before the affair occurred. We easily discovered issues that needed examination and around which behavior changes were needed. One was that they both wanted more passionate sex, and this was easily addressed since both genuinely wanted it. Some standard sex therapy exercises were really all they needed to regain their old more sensual selves with each other.

> To live a more principled life requires, among other things, the ability to at least delay the immediate gratification of particular emotional wants and wishes and sometimes put them off entirely.

The other focus was on character issues. The kind of questions I used to get into this were: Apart from who your partner is and how he or she behaves, how do you want to live your life? What kind of a person do you want to be? In his case, given the ongoing availability of the other woman who still wanted him as a lover, and the same temptation, how would he decide what to do? Would he be able to stick with a decision to stay with his wife? Did he really want to? We discussed this at length.

We looked at his own growing-up and family experience. As an only child, he said he was somewhat "spoiled" and "indulged." He was not always held to account for the things he had agreed to do. At the same time, he found his mother emotionally "controlling" and not accepting of who he was even as an adult. He learned not to be open with her and to appear to be what she wanted. To some extent he had been experiencing his wife in the same way, and behaving with her in the same way.

As a part of the therapy, he began to make trips home to visit his parents and work at being more of a real, solid self with them. Even though there had never been any significant open conflict in his family, he found this extremely difficult to do. He hated being "a disappointment" to them, but he told them about his affair and other aspects of who he was that he knew they would not like or appreciate. He worried less about their reactions and focused more on how he wanted to be with them. He began to feel much more comfortable living within his own skin and being the person he wanted to be. He reported being better able to define himself within his congregation as well, and less willing to hide his true beliefs when he knew they wouldn't fit with some of his members' beliefs.

Anxiety and delayed gratification

To live a more principled life requires, among other things, the ability to at least delay the immediate gratification of particular emotional wants and wishes and sometimes put them off entirely. This includes the ability to tolerate our anxiety over possibly not having or ever getting what we want from others or from life. Although we might feel happier in the short term, seeking gratification of moment-by-moment emotional wants and wishes leads to an erratic and less happy life in the long run, and much poorer relationships in both love and friendship.

This was the case with the clergyman husband above. As a young person, he would secretly do things he wanted to do without letting his parents know. Of course, some degree of this is normal. However, this became a lifestyle with him. He maintained a pleasing façade with them, and they didn't really hold him to account when his shortcomings did become evident. They let things slide. He decided that was the way to live. As it turned out, he had had two previous affairs in his marriage and he had felt "emotionally entitled" to them. They were his due, his compensation, for being a good boy, appearing to be what others wanted him to be.

It seems this is not an unusual attitude among those apparently good people who go bad. Recent research suggests that some highly moral people are liable to go wrong if they think their goodness gives them the right to cheat in some form. Based on the self-report of about three hundred office managers and students who think they are highly moral, the researchers found they admitted to cutting ethical corners of all sorts because they were otherwise good people. They felt entitled as a kind of reward for being good.

Anxiety can develop when we don't get what we want or when we think that we should have something. A wife may scheme a way to get a new, expensive dress without letting her "stingy" husband find out. Her anxiety around not having the dress turns into a need. She justifies this as a right in return for whatever service she provides him. This leads her to be dishonest with her husband and to lose respect for him. Having the good feelings she gets with the dress, how she looks and what that does for her, and the admiration of her friends becomes more important to her. Austen might have called it her vanity. But there is a clear, underlying emotional need that she is addressing and reacting to. Her anxiety grows if she doesn't get the dress. But would she want her husband to behave the same way with her? No, not likely.

Henry Crawford's vanity (*Mansfield Park*) cannot stand it when attractive women do not immediately respond to his charms. He feels good when he has their admiration and affection. In his own anxious state he needs the "fix" of their attraction to him. Without that fix he feels personally threatened. He takes after his own guardian's similar bad behavior, which he observed while growing up. Thus he feels compelled to pursue Maria (Bertram) Rushworth when she is cool toward him at a party, and he destroys his possible happy future with Fanny Price. We read (italics mine) in chapter 48:

> Henry Crawford, ruined by early independence and bad domestic example, indulged in the freaks of a cold-blooded vanity a little too long. . . .
>
> Had he done as he intended, and as he knew he ought, by going down to Everingham after his return from Portsmouth, he might have been deciding his own happy destiny. But he was pressed to stay for Mrs. Fraser's party; his staying was made of flattering consequence, and he was to meet Mrs. Rushworth there. Curiosity and vanity were both engaged, and *the temptation of immediate pleasure was too strong for a mind unused to make any sacrifice to right*: he resolved to defer his Norfolk journey, resolved that writing should answer the purpose of it, or that its purpose was unimportant, and staid. He saw Mrs. Rushworth, was received by her with a coldness which ought to have been repulsive, and have established apparent indifference between them for ever; but he was mortified, he could not bear to be thrown off by the woman whose smiles had been so wholly at his command: he must exert himself to subdue so proud a display of resentment; it was anger on Fanny's account; he must get the better of it, and make Mrs. Rushworth Maria Bertram again in her treatment of himself.
>
> When he returned from Richmond, he would have been glad to see Mrs. Rushworth no more. All that followed was the result of

her imprudence; and he went off with her at last, because he could
not help it, regretting Fanny even at the moment, but regretting her
infinitely more when all the bustle of the intrigue was over, and a
very few months had taught him, by the force of contrast, to place
a yet higher value on the sweetness of her temper, the purity of her
mind, and the excellence of her principles.

Not many playboys of Henry's sort find their way into therapy. If
Henry had been able to seriously focus on improving his character, then
he would have been a good candidate for therapy. As the love of a good
woman can often do for a person like him, Fanny had had some impact
on him, but it was not enough to get him to truly want to change. His
life with whomever he eventually does marry is going to be a chaotic and
unhappy one. As Austen says, he will deeply regret losing a woman of
Fanny's principled goodness.

Willoughby, in *Sense and Sensibility*, is another example of a less principled lover who focuses more on the pleasure of the moment. If he wants
the attentions of a beautiful woman, he pursues her, regardless of other
commitments. He develops a lifestyle of getting what he wants, when
he wants it (a new carriage—the equivalent of a fancy new car today—
hunting horses and dogs, or guns). He acquires these things without any
thought of how he will pay for them. If it brings him pleasure, he gets these
toys without considering anything else. He knows that his debts and the
lifestyle he desires necessitate that he marry a wealthy woman, not a much
poorer woman like Marianne. This need takes precedence over whether
he loves the woman he marries or not. These are all things that Marianne,
who allows herself to be seduced by his attentions, does not recognize.

Toward the end of the book, in chapter 47, when all the facts have
been made known to Marianne, and after Willoughby's confession to
Elinor, the two women discuss Willoughby and Marianne's relationship to
him. Elinor is congratulating Marianne for the greater clarity of her thinking, and this discussion continues to help Marianne think things through
(again the italics are mine).

> "You consider the matter," said Elinor, "exactly as a good mind
> and a sound understanding must consider it; and I dare say you per-
> ceive . . . that your marriage must have involved you in many cer-
> tain troubles and disappointments, in which you would have been

poorly supported by an affection, on his side, much less certain. Had you married, you must have been always poor. His expensiveness is acknowledged even by himself; and *his whole conduct declares, that self-denial is a word hardly understood by him.* His demands, and your inexperience together, on a small, very small income, must have brought on distresses which would not be the less grievous to you, from having been entirely unknown and unthought of before. Your sense of honour and honesty would have led you, I know, when aware of your situation, to attempt all the economy that would appear to you possible . . . had you endeavoured, however reasonably, to abridge his enjoyments, is it not to be feared, that instead of prevailing on feelings so selfish to consent to it, you would have lessened your own influence on his heart, and made him regret the connection which had involved him in such difficulties?"

Marianne's lips quivered, and she repeated the word "selfish" in a tone that implied, "Do you really think him selfish?"

"The whole of his behaviour," replied Elinor, "from the beginning to the end of the affair, has been grounded on selfishness. It was selfishness which first made him sport with your affections; which afterwards, when his own were engaged, made him delay the confession of it, and which finally carried him from Barton. *His own enjoyment, or his own ease, was, in every particular, his ruling principle.*"

Willoughby is such a modern guy. Many young female clients complained that they only met guys like him. I asked them, "Whether you meet a guy in a pub or in church, how can you determine whether you have met a guy who is going to be faithful, caring, and honest in his relationship with you? Can you tell this simply by whether he is handsome, lively, fun, interesting, and so forth?" The intent of these kinds of questions was to ask them about their own values, beliefs, standards, or principles, and how they would discover and evaluate those of others. Of course, this is not an easy project.

Mary Crawford (*Mansfield Park*), Henry's sister, is the most ambiguous of Austen's "bad" characters. So skillfully has Austen portrayed her that we really have to think about her character. We understand why Edmund fell for her. Most of us like her more than Fanny Price. Austen's own family members liked her more than Fanny Price. Like Willoughby, she is exemplary of a certain type of modern woman. She comes off as so attractive, accomplished, charming, and witty that Fanny pales in comparison. Austen, though, subtly shows where her deep, basic shortcomings are and then has Edmund and Fanny openly discuss this "perversion of mind" at the end of the story. Edmund reports that Mary's true character and her "faults of principle" are finally revealed to him in that Mary does not believe the affair between Maria and her brother Henry is anything more than "folly," and the chief difficulty with it lay only in their being discovered by others.

Mary blames Fanny's refusal of Henry's proposal of marriage for creating the situation in which Henry ran off with Maria. She makes excuses for her brother, saying that if Fanny had accepted Henry, then his affair with Maria would not have happened; she says it would "only" have led to annual affairs with her or meetings in some holiday place. Edmund does not see Mary's moral failure as just a personal "cruelty" as Fanny claims. Rather than "faults of temper," he says, "Hers are faults of principle." As Edmund says in chapter 47:

> Cruelty, do you call it? We differ there. No, hers is not a cruel nature. I do not consider her as meaning to wound my feelings. The evil lies yet deeper: in her total ignorance, unsuspiciousness of there being such feelings; in a perversion of mind which made it natural to her to treat the subject as she did. She was speaking only as she had been used to hear others speak, as she imagined everybody else would speak. Hers are not faults of temper. She would not voluntarily give unnecessary pain to any one. . . . Hers are faults of principle, Fanny; of blunted delicacy and a corrupted, vitiated mind.

Being aware that our character is not all that we want it to be and needs strengthening is an important first step in developing it. Mary lacked this awareness. As a child she lacked a good role model who could help train her. She never had certain important principles held up to her as goals to be aspired to. Edmund says she is not even aware of lacking them. Mary feels no shame or embarrassment or defensiveness about her character for this reason. She is just being the way she was trained to be by her aunt and uncle.

The goodness in your family and developing your own

Do you have any role models, any heroes for goodness in your life? Are there people in your family who have done a good job of living a more principled life? Most of us have at least one or two people in our extended family who could be like the more heroic Austen type person; people who have faced difficult circumstances with for-
titude, good spirits, wise judgments, and a grace or style that kept them in good relationships with others in the

> You need to focus on how you get "trig-
> gered" into forgetting your own goals
> and passively get caught up in reacting
> to the actions of others or going along
> with their unprincipled actions.

process. If they don't exist in your family, then there may be others who might model these qualities for you, for example, friends, acquaintances, teachers, or bosses. There are many good people in the world. Seek them out and learn from them.

You might try to get to know these people better. Could you interview them, asking questions along these lines: Would you help me with some-
thing I am thinking about? You know, I have always thought of you as a good person. I have wondered how you got that way. What sort of people and events have influenced you or made an impact on you? Who have you looked up to in life? Did they say or do anything that was particularly helpful for you? Did you ever think consciously about being good, or did it just come automatically? Do you remember struggling with any of it before? What has been (or is) your biggest struggle? Was there a turning point for you? How did you deal with it? How did you arrive at your own standards of goodness? What are your principles for living? Where did they come from? What advice would you give to someone who wants to live a more principled life?

The questions you can ask are endless. These are only suggestions. The conversation will feel awkward because no one talks about these things anymore. But the person you are interviewing will, after some probable initial hesitation and likely expressions of humility, begin to appreciate your serious interest and the resulting opportunity to think about these things with you.

As a second step, it is essential to begin the process of defining your own principles for living and to actively pursue embodying them in your life in the midst of trying circumstances or difficult relationship experiences. What do you have to do to remind yourself of this task and what

virtues might be required in specific situations? They are truly *your principles* only when you act on them in specific situations. If you are not acting on them, then you are simply fooling yourself.

Next, you need to focus on how you get "triggered" into forgetting your own goals and passively get caught up in reacting to the actions of others or going along with their unprincipled actions. What behavior in others sets you off and gives rise to unprincipled behavior? You can then focus on interrupting your automatic reactions. The age-old advice to "count to ten before responding" is really a worthwhile suggestion.

At first you may have to rehearse new responses in your own mind, thinking through scenarios and seeing yourself being different and saying different things. Then you begin to practice these alternative, more principled responses in actual situations. Practice does make perfect. Each little accomplishment in overcoming a bit of reactivity on your part will become another stone in building a stronger, firmer character foundation.

Here is one little technique. Could you imagine yourself, as you go through the day (or a week), wearing a T-shirt under your regular clothes that had printed on it a word such as *amiable, kind, generous, civil, thoughtful, courageous,* or *faithful*; and then try to live up to the word in your daily interactions? With each day or week, you would have a new T-shirt and a new goal for that period of time. In each situation you encounter, what might that virtue look like in action? You could set out to practice that particular virtue in all of your interactions. A review at the end of each day, looking at the events of the day, could help you think about how you did and how you could improve. In this way you would build new habits.

Initially your awareness of failing to live by your principles in these circumstances will be after the fact. Only in reflecting later on your actions and comparing them to your more principled goals for yourself will you discover what got in the way. Might there have been a better way to behave in specific situations? What would it have taken for you to have done it? Working at these things on a day-by-day basis will, over time, make a significant difference.

❧ Eleven ❧

Critical Principles
in Relationships

Taking a principled stand

People of good character and emotional maturity are usually enjoyable, interesting, and helpful people to be around. They normally demonstrate the virtue of being amiable. They contribute to the life of a group and help to make things go well in relationships. They are generally well liked and dependable: they do what they say they will do, and they are open and clear about what they will not do. They are thoughtful and can help others think through the issues they face in their own lives. By and large, they are considerate, caring, and compassionate.

However, on important matters, they do not always do what others expect of them or want them to do. Such times may be relatively rare in their relationships, but at those times they will not go along with the crowd just for the sake of being a part of the group, or go against their own principles in order to please others or gain their acceptance. In spite of their caring, they do not exist to make others happy with them. At these times, it may seem to others that they are inconsiderate because they are not compliant or willing to do what others want at critical junctures. People of good character may be required, from time to time, to take a principled stand even in opposition to friends and family.

> People of good character may be required, from time to time, to take a principled stand even in opposition to friends and family.

Elizabeth Bennet (*Sense and Sensibility*) can see the silliness of some of her mother's attitudes and positions. She does not make an issue of them nor ever reprove her mother. She simply does not let herself be guided by her mother's stances on certain issues. Without making it a big issue, she ignores Mrs. Bennet's objections to walking to the Netherfield household where her sister Jane is laid up sick. Mrs. Bennet wants to give Jane lots of time alone with Mr. Bingley. While Elizabeth understands what her mother is up to, she is genuinely concerned about her sister's health and insists on going to visit her.

Many of the wives I have worked with in therapy have had to take principled stands on their own behalf within their marriages and families. Many of them married at a time when women were more subservient. Like Stepford Wives, they were expected to run a household that was designed for the comfort and pleasure of the "hardworking" husband. This was their role. In the 1970s and '80s, women who had married within this earlier cultural framework began to rethink their lives. Even if they had begun to work outside of the home, they were still expected to run the household as they had before. This essential unfairness became a critical issue in many marriages.

Many mature husbands got it when their wives presented them with this issue. They knew immediately that things must change and that they would have to participate more fully in all of the duties of running a family and a household. They were not simply the guests at an inn that existed for their pleasure and comfort and provided them a retreat from the rigors of having a "full-time job."

Many husbands, however, either didn't understand or resisted doing so. Quite a few marriages came apart simply because the husbands refused to even consider changing their ways. Their wives left them. Other wives were so ambivalent about the changes they wanted to make that they could never effectively present their case or take a stand. This ambivalence allowed their husbands to continue their lifestyle while arguing about the "unreasonableness" of their wife's position. These wives were waiting for their husband's approval before they could change. Often years in an unhappy relationship passed before any changes were made. Simply complaining and arguing about the way things were usually did nothing more than stir the pot of boiling domestic unhappiness. It did not work to just wait for these husbands to comply or agree to cooperate in making changes.

In these situations, the women who clarified their positions (first for themselves), confidently made them known in the family, and then acted on them achieved the best outcomes. They did not depend on the support and cooperation of others. They simply took action for themselves. The women who were unhappy with their lives as homemakers went out and got the education they wanted and the job they wanted. They did not continue to do all of what they had been doing in the home. Only at this point, after the women acted on what they would and would not do, did some husbands begin to come around, which allowed these couples to negotiate a more reasonable home arrangement. Usually these marriages went on to happier times.

I recently attended my fiftieth high school reunion, class of 1957. More than sixty of us wrote brief biographies of our lives since high school. What many of us ended up doing in life was amazing and unpredictable. Back in the '50s most of us were just out to have fun. Many of the women had developed careers. I was impressed with the stories of how many had to struggle with and break through male-erected barriers in order to move ahead in their workplace. Often to achieve their goals, they had to take principled stands that amounted to "What I am asking for is fair and no different from what the men are getting, so either this happens or I am out of here." They were usually too valuable to lose so they got what they were asking for.

Let me give you an example from my own marriage of a wife taking a principled stand. What is the most common gift a husband gives his wife on their wedding day? The answer is, "His mother." I did this. I had kept a significant amount of distance from my mother (who had been a single parent for me, an only child) through my young adult years. Without us ever talking about it when we married, Lois automatically took up the primary job of corresponding and talking on the phone with my mother. I thought this was great. But in the second year of marriage, she said to me, "You know, I have a mother of my own. I don't need two. I am no longer going to be responsible for calling your mother, or remembering her birthday, or sending cards. And I am not even going to remind you that these things ought to be done. I am not going to think about it at all." It was a simple announcement, not an angry attack. Neither was she seeking to get my consent before she did it. She just did it without rancor or blame or any negative feelings.

Many wives know automatically what a difficult stance this would be to take. There are huge emotional pressures on wives to be in charge of all extended family affairs. Doing so is commonly understood to be a wife's responsibility. Lois would be seen as shirking a major responsibility in the family, even by my mother.

Her announcement of this decision turned out to be the easier part of her effort. For the next two years I did nothing in relation to my mother except to call her at Christmastime and for her birthday. Essentially our side of the family did not initiate contact with her. Lois knew that she would be seen as failing as a wife, but she said nothing to me or anyone and did not relent on her decision. She did not nag me about the absence of cards and phone calls. Nothing. The issue was closed for her. She stood by her decision. Eventually I saw that she was serious and was not going to relent out of the emotional pressure of guilt. I finally began to take responsibility for the relationship with my mother, and that was the beginning of a slow-to-come but significant positive shift for me with her. It would not likely have happened if Lois had continued to take responsibility for that relationship.

> It is not always easy to maintain a particular principled position when those we care about, and think are our friends, oppose us.

Over the (now forty) years of marriage, if I proved unwilling to talk about some issue in the marriage, Lois would simply tell me what she would and would not do in response. I began to believe her and took it seriously. If I thought I had a case for my side, she would talk with me about it and maybe we could negotiate something different. She is quite considerate and reasonable and listens to what I say. But most often I saw the reasonableness of her position and knew that I was going to have to change my behavior if I wanted to stay married to her, which I did.

Lois is generous in spirit, humble and not proud, caring and compassionate. We do not often think of such people as also being strong and willing to take stands, but that is how she is. She does it without rancor. I know that once she has thought something through, she is not likely to change her stand unless new information arises. Then she can be flexible and change her position.

It is not always easy to maintain a particular principled position when those we care about, and think are our friends, oppose us. In *Northanger Abbey*, John and Isabella Thorpe pressure young Catherine Morland to abandon her walking engagement with the Tilneys and to join their group for a carriage trip to Clifton to see Blaize Castle. Isabella first tries flattery and then accuses Catherine of hurting her, both of which fail to dissuade Catherine. The three following passages are all from chapter 13.

> She had that moment settled with Miss Tilney to take their proposed walk tomorrow; it was quite determined, and she would

not, upon any account, retract. But that she must and should retract was instantly the eager cry of both the Thorpes; they must go to Clifton tomorrow, they would not go without her, it would be nothing to put off a mere walk for one day longer, and they would not hear of a refusal. Catherine was distressed, but not subdued. "Do not urge me, Isabella. I am engaged to [go with] Miss Tilney. I cannot go." This availed nothing. The same arguments assailed her again; she must go, she should go, and they would not hear of a refusal. "It would be so easy to tell Miss Tilney that you had just been reminded of a prior engagement, and must only beg to put off the walk till Tuesday."

"No, it would not be easy. I could not do it. There has been no prior engagement." But Isabella became only more and more urgent, calling on her in the most affectionate manner, addressing her by the most endearing names. She was sure her dearest, sweetest Catherine would not seriously refuse such a trifling request to a friend who loved her so dearly. . . . But all in vain; Catherine felt herself to be in the right, and though pained by such tender, such flattering supplication, could not allow it to influence her. Isabella then tried another method. She reproached her with having more affection for Miss Tilney, though she had known her so little a while, than for her best and oldest friends, with being grown cold and indifferent, in short, towards herself. "I cannot help being jealous, Catherine, when I see myself slighted for strangers, I, who love you so excessively! . . . and to see myself supplanted in your friendship by strangers does cut me to the quick, I own."

Catherine does not give in. Then Catherine's own brother, James, joins in with the others and the pressure on her increases. They accuse her of stubbornness and obstinacy.

The three others still continued together, walking in a most uncomfortable manner to poor Catherine; sometimes not a word was said, sometimes she was again attacked with supplications or reproaches, and her arm was still linked within Isabella's, though their hearts were at war. At one moment she was softened, at another irritated; always distressed, but always steady.

"I did not think you had been so obstinate, Catherine," said James; "you were not used to be so hard to persuade; you once were the kindest, best-tempered of my sisters."

"I hope I am not less so now," she replied, very feelingly; "but indeed I cannot go. If I am wrong, I am doing what I believe to be right."

Then Isabella's brother, John Thorpe, tries to trick her into going with a lie by saying that he has just made excuses to the Tilneys for her. She sees the lie and still refuses to be persuaded. All of this is not easy for young Catherine. She is anxious over the disapproval of her friends and has to examine her behavior. Her reflections convince her that she has behaved honorably and that she has demonstrated good character in sticking to her position and in not succumbing to the immediate gratification of visiting Blaize Castle at Clifton.

Away walked Catherine in great agitation, as fast as the crowd would permit her, fearful of being pursued, yet determined to persevere. As she walked, she reflected on what had passed. It was painful to her to disappoint and displease them, particularly to displease her brother; but she could not repent her resistance. Setting her own inclination apart, to have failed a second time in her engagement to Miss Tilney, to have retracted a promise voluntarily made only five minutes before, and on a false pretence too, must have been wrong. She had not been withstanding them on selfish principles alone, she had not consulted merely her own gratification; that might have been ensured in some degree by the excursion itself, by seeing Blaize Castle; no, she had attended to what was due to others, and to her own character in their opinion.

Inwardly, Catherine is irritated and distressed by their accusations and attacks, but she does not relent. She stands by her principles. She is steady. Whenever we take a stand that others do not like, we can count on them to test it and to push us to give in and go along. All sorts of unjust accusations might be made. It usually does not avail to plead for their cooperation. It is essential that we not react, get defensive, argue, or go on the counterattack. All of these responses simply encourage others to keep at us. We can listen to their positions for any sign of reasonableness, or for something we have not considered, and possibly even change our minds as a result, but otherwise we need to stay on course, stay "steady."

Henry Tilney takes a similar stand with his father when he learns of the circumstances that led General Tilney abruptly to order Catherine to leave Northanger Abbey and send her home to Fullerton, alone and without an escort. Women were not encouraged to take long coach rides on their own. The general's rude and ungracious behavior resulted primarily from learning that Catherine's family did not have the kind of money he had been led to believe by John Thorpe. Henry goes to visit Catherine to make sure she arrived home safely, to explain and apologize for his father's behavior, and to ask for Catherine's hand if she will still have him. All of this he does against his father's will. Henry acts out of honorable principle, as well as love, and the general is clearly behaving dishonorably. In chapter 30 Austen tells us about Henry's principled stand with his father.

> Henry, in having such things to relate [to Catherine] of his father, was almost as pitiable as in their first avowal to himself. He blushed for the narrow-minded counsel which he was obliged to expose. The conversation between them at Northanger had been of the most unfriendly kind. Henry's indignation on hearing how Catherine had been treated, on comprehending his father's views, and being ordered to acquiesce in them, had been open and bold. The general, accustomed on every ordinary occasion to give the law in his family, prepared for no reluctance but of feeling, no opposing desire that should dare to clothe itself in words, could ill brook the opposition of his son, steady as the sanction of reason and the dictate of conscience could make it. But, in such a cause, his anger, though it must shock, could not intimidate Henry, who was sustained in his purpose by a conviction of its justice. He felt himself bound as much in honour as in affection to Miss Morland, and believing that heart to be his own which he had been directed to gain, no unworthy retraction of a tacit consent, no reversing decree of unjustifiable anger, could shake his fidelity, or influence the resolutions it prompted.

The general had been expecting obedience from his son and expected to receive "no reluctance but of feeling." He did not care that Henry might feel anger or resentment; these were meaningless in terms of actual behavior, and would eventually pass. He was used to his children being upset with his decisions. This did not affect him or cause him to change his position. The general's behavior was stimulated by greed, while Henry's came out of love and principle. He was in the right.

The most famous example in Austen's work of a hero taking a principled stand is the one Elizabeth Bennet takes with Lady Catherine De Bourgh in *Pride and Prejudice*. Lady Catherine makes a surprise visit to the Bennets as soon as she hears that her nephew Darcy intends to propose marriage to Elizabeth. She commands Elizabeth to turn him down and uses every trick she can muster to pressure and shame Elizabeth into promising to refuse Darcy if he does propose. They have a wonderful argument in which all of Austen's art is brought to bear. She shows us the kind of clear thinking, personal authority, and courage Elizabeth needs in taking a principled stand. Here is only part of the argument in chapter 56. Having barged into the Bennet home, Lady Catherine demands:

> "Tell me once for all, are you engaged to him?"
>
> Though Elizabeth would not, for the mere purpose of obliging Lady Catherine, have answered this question, she could not but say, after a moment's deliberation,
>
> "I am not."
>
> Lady Catherine seemed pleased.
>
> "And will you promise me, never to enter into such an engagement?"
>
> "I will make no promise of the kind."
>
> "Miss Bennet I am shocked and astonished. I expected to find a more reasonable young woman. But do not deceive yourself into a belief that I will ever recede. I shall not go away till you have given me the assurance I require."
>
> "And I certainly never shall give it. I am not to be intimidated into anything so wholly unreasonable. Your ladyship wants Mr. Darcy to marry your daughter; but would my giving you the wished-for promise make their marriage at all more probable? Supposing him to be attached to me, would my refusing to accept his hand make him wish to bestow it on his cousin? . . . You have widely mistaken my character, if you think I can be worked on by such persuasions as these . . ."
>
> "Not so hasty, if you please. I have by no means done. To all the objections I have already urged, I have still another to add. I

am no stranger to the particulars of your youngest sister's infamous elopement. I know it all; that the young man's marrying her was a patched-up business, at the expense of your father and uncles. And is *such* a girl to be my nephew's sister? Is *her* husband, is the son of his late father's steward, to be his brother? Heaven and earth!—of what are you thinking? Are the shades of Pemberley to be thus polluted?"

"You can *now* have nothing farther to say," she resentfully answered. "You have insulted me in every possible method. I must beg to return to the house."

And she rose as she spoke. Lady Catherine rose also, and they turned back. Her ladyship was highly incensed.

"You have no regard, then, for the honour and credit of my nephew! Unfeeling, selfish girl! Do you not consider that a connection with you must disgrace him in the eyes of everybody?"

"Lady Catherine, I have nothing farther to say. You know my sentiments."

"You are then resolved to have him?"

"I have said no such thing. I am only resolved to act in that manner, which will, in my own opinion, constitute my happiness, without reference to you, or to any person so wholly unconnected with me."

Elizabeth (and Austen) is saying that the wishes and wants of people she is connected with are more taken into consideration by her. She does not take her principled stands in some kind of moral vacuum. She lives within a community of people to whom she has obligations and for whom she cares. So later, when she tells her father of her wish to marry Darcy, seeking his approval, she behaves quite differently in response to his opposition. He has not been privy to the development of her own thinking and feeling about Darcy over time. So she tells her father about how her loving feelings have developed. What he thinks is important to her, and she respects his opinion, as he does hers. He has some authority over her still, and he respectfully questions her change of position and asks if she has carefully thought through this decision. Unlike many fathers, he did not want her marrying Darcy simply for his money.

There are many examples in Austen of her heroes taking such principled stands. Edward Ferrars, in *Sense and Sensibility*, takes a costly stand with his mother around whom he will marry, and she actually disowns him from the family fortune. Each one of Austen's novels pivots on such determined and honorable behavior. Her heroes regularly take principled positions on critical issues that go against the wishes, wants, or commands of others. They do not intend to be defiant or rebellious—that is not their goal; they intend only to behave honorably, in accordance with their values, when such behavior is not thought convenient, desirable, advantageous, or comfortable by others.

Standing alone

Exercising what Austen called "the resolution of a collected mind" can have significant consequences for us in our relationships. Family and friends may well attempt to punish us for our principled stand, by whatever means, in order to get us to conform to their wishes and wants. They are in effect saying, "You are unreasonable, obstinate, and selfish. If you don't do what we want, there will be unpleasant consequences for you. We will make you pay. Change back to how you were and do what we want, or else."

One client told me about his growing up in a European village of two thousand people. His friends were quite "provincial" minded, he said,

Jane Austen's heroes frequently find themselves in circumstances in which they must take a principled stand in spite of the resistance, opposition, and even anger of those (often family or close friends) who want them to choose otherwise. They are good people—even when their good behavior is not appreciated by others.

They take their stand not out of petulance, defiance, or mean-spiritedness, but rather out of personal integrity—the need to be true to their principles of living.

- *Reflect on your relationships with family, friends, and colleagues. Are there any areas in any of these relationships where you feel the need to take a principled stand that others might resist or find uncomfortable?*

- *What are the likely consequences of taking such a stand for you? For others?*

THIS ABOVE ALL, TO YOUR OWN SELF BE TRUE. — SHAKESPEARE

and could not see a life for themselves outside of their village. He had educational and financial goals that went beyond village life. When they were buying their first cars, he was still riding a bicycle. He told them he was saving money for university. They laughed at him and said, "Who do you think you are? Some big shot or something?" Their attitudes hurt him, but he stuck to his goals. Although he remained friendly toward them, they began to shun him and have less to do with him, saying, "He thinks he's different from us." He eventually moved to Canada and, achieving his goals, became successful at what he wanted to do. While I was working with him, he made his first trip ever back to his home village and visited with some of these old friends and relatives. They no longer laughed at him; they congratulated him on his achievements.

> Significant changes in relationships usually do not come about until one person is willing to risk the loss of the relationship.

When taking a principled stand, we do not set out to be alone. We want to live in close contact with others and enjoy the mutuality of warm relationships with them. But if we fear being alone and cannot live independently on our own, then the threat of punishment and being cut off from them will be effective and we will give up self and abandon our principles to maintain connection at any price. If my client thought he "needed" the acceptance of his friends and could not live without it, he would not have created the kind of life he wanted. Like them, he would have stayed stuck in his village. Many a husband or wife has failed to take a principled stand in their marriage simply because they feared the loss of their partner if they did. This fear is understandable, but significant changes in relationships usually do not come about until one person is willing to risk the loss of the relationship.

Here is an example with a twist. The wife in a couple I began to see told me, in an individual session, that her friends were strongly against her doing marital counseling. Over the years, she had told them a lot about the pain she had experienced in her marriage due to her husband's behavior. They told her she "shouldn't take it anymore" and that she should leave him. This is what several of them had done in their marriages.

She told them that she couldn't leave him until she believed she had given the marriage the best shot she could for succeeding. Over time and with lots of hard work, the couple's life together gradually improved to the point where both were quite satisfied with their progress. But she had to make new friends. Her old friends were sure she was lying about how much better it was and they distanced from her. She decided that they hadn't really been good friends. They needed her to agree with them and be like them in order to be close.

One of the challenges of being newly divorced is being alone. People who were divorced by their partner may already have compromised essential parts of themselves over the years in order not to lose their partner, and still it didn't work. Often their fear is based on the fact that they have never lived alone, having moved from their parents' house, or a college dorm, or an apartment with a roommate to life with their partner. I talked with them in therapy about how being single would give them a chance to get to know themselves better and be more comfortable being alone. When people accomplish this, they are less likely to be threatened if a new partner says some version of "Do this or else I am leaving." I discouraged these clients from jumping into new relationships too early out of their fear of being alone, before they learned more about themselves, their own standards and expectations in relationships, and how they could improve their ability to choose a potential partner.

All of Austen's heroes suffer some version of these pressures to conform and threats about what will happen if they don't. Occasionally the threats are fulfilled. The most obvious example is Fanny Price (*Mansfield Park*). First, her refusal to act in the play brought a certain amount of isolation. She was punished with distance, silence, and anger. However, the group was too dependent on her to fully isolate themselves from her.

More significantly, she is punished because of her refusal to marry Henry Crawford. She has major misgivings about his character and values. Sir Thomas sends her away from Mansfield Park. She is cut off from those who have been her adopted family and goes back home to her poor, unhappy, and chaotic birth family in Portsmouth. Sir Thomas wishes to punish her for refusing what he thinks is a great opportunity. He believes he is acting in her interest. Eventually, for various reasons, all who hear of her refusal join in the punishment. Her courage and integrity are severely put to the test. Nevertheless, she maintains her stance without giving a full explanation to anyone as to why she is refusing Henry's proposal. Here is part of Sir Thomas's reprimand to her in chapter 32:

> I had thought you peculiarly free from willfulness of temper, self-conceit, and every tendency to that independence of spirit

which prevails so much in modern days, even in young women, and which in young women is offensive and disgusting beyond all common offence. But you have now shewn me that you can be willful and perverse; that you can and will decide for yourself, without any consideration or deference for those who have surely some right to guide you, without even asking their advice. You have shewn yourself very, very different from anything that I had imagined. The advantage or disadvantage of your family, of your parents, your brothers and sisters, never seems to have had a moment's share in your thoughts on this occasion. How *they* might be benefited, how *they* must rejoice in such an establishment for you, is nothing to *you*. You think only of yourself.

There is incredible pressure on Fanny. She is charged with being willful, uncaring of others, ungrateful, and selfish. Of course, none of these accusations are true of her. In truth she is resisting the patriarchal authority of the father figure. Very often, when principled people take their stands, they are charged with "selfishness" because they will not do what others want. Taking a principled stand can have a cost attached. However, as long as we do not waver in our position and do whatever we can to maintain friendly contact with those who have distanced themselves, not reacting to their reactions or trying to defend and justify ourselves, they will usually renew contact at some point and concede to the principled position. In Fanny's case it took months before her critics changed their position, but they did come around quite quickly once they discovered how right she was to refuse Henry on the basis of his character.

Even though they had agreed with Sir Thomas in pressuring Fanny to marry Henry, nearly everyone at Mansfield (except Mrs. Norris) was happy when he invited Fanny back. She came back as a much more respected person with much greater influence because people agreed she was the only one to see what they had missed with regard to the character of both Henry and Mary Crawford.

If we become anxious about our principled stand, or try to reason and argue people into agreeing with us, or react to their emotional statements with our own emotionality, or try to punish them for punishing us, then nothing will change. The basic emotional process remains the same. This is important and essential. Arguing with our critics only sends the message, "I am unsure of my position and need you to agree with me so I can feel comfortable acting on it." They will only take stronger stands with us and be more punishing. We have to have a way to deal with our anxiety about being left alone or abandoned, and not collapse or give in to the emotional process involved. We simply get on with our lives as best we can with what we have. We don't focus on the attackers and what they are doing, or how unfair they are, or whatever.

Assuming we are otherwise well connected to those involved, taking principled stands is the way our emotional systems change and begin to function more effectively or at a higher level. This is what happened at Mansfield Park as various family members, beginning with Sir Thomas, began to recognize their own errors. Emotional systems have a certain homeostatic level or balance in their functioning, which tends to keep things the same no matter how quiet or intense the process. Someone behaving significantly differently is a threat to the continued functioning of the system as it is. It is normal for people in the system to get anxious and react with some sort of critical or punishing behavior when a person takes a principled stand that does not go along with the system as it is.

Arguing and emotional reactivity do not change this process. If Fanny had argued with Sir Thomas, telling him he was wrong, unfair, blind, and dictatorial, she would have gotten nowhere and only intensified his own beliefs and feelings about her. I might have tried to argue with Lois around her "abandonment" of my mother, but given her emotional maturity and resolve, it would have done no good. If she had attacked me for being a terrible son and insisted that she was not going to cover for me anymore, I would probably have been defensive and gone on the counterattack. If she had cried and argued with me, wanting my approval, and tried to convince me of the correctness of her position, her cause would have been lost. She would have been saying in effect, "I can't change until you agree with me and give me permission to take this position." And this would have kept both of us stuck.

Someone has to step outside of the normal emotional process and simply behave differently for change to happen. A typical argument in today's modern parlance would be along the lines of "You are not respecting my feelings!" If Fanny had been a typical daughter who argued and yelled and screamed with some version of this, and cried at her father's demands, but ultimately resentfully gave in, nothing would have changed. As is said of General Tilney in relation to Henry, he was "prepared for no reluctance but of feeling." Henry's being upset and angry did not bother him. Expressing feelings does not usually change things. It just heats things up. Only behavior changes things. Making clear statements of what you will and will not do, based on principle, and then acting accordingly, is what leads to change.

Most of the time something as dramatic as Fanny's expulsion from Mansfield Park is an unlikely outcome. This was extreme. Normally when people take a principled stand, the upset and reaction will be of a lesser intensity and a shorter duration. It depends on how much the usual functioning of the emotional system is being challenged. In Fanny's case, she was viewed as an ungrateful rebel for refusing to recognize the absolute authority of the father and disobeying him. Sir Thomas recognized that not being Fanny's actual father diminished his ability to demand obedience, but not by a lot. Fathers back then had the right to arrange marriages and say whom a daughter would marry. They also had the right to punish disobedience however they chose, as demonstrated later in the devastating exile of his daughter Maria and Mrs. Norris.

> Expressing feelings does not usually change things. It just heats things up. Only behavior changes things.

It takes a significant amount of emotional maturity to define a self and be different within the emotional systems we are a part of. We change and grow through the exercise of our own individuality; through the clarification of our goals, values, and principles; and through our confident belief in them. And this is the way the emotional systems we are a part of grow and change as well. It is heroic work and difficult work that takes courage. People who are willing to do it, however, improve their lives in general and their relationships in particular.

ℰ Twelve ℬ

Bringing It All Together

Six essential points

In this next to last chapter, I want to review the essential points of my argument for becoming the best people we can be and offer further illustrations of what I mean. I will first list six essential points and then refer to them by number in the examples that follow. The points below are not sequential in terms of order of development; they are not a step-by-step plan for how to grow. They are interrelated because we may work at one of them and then another in no particular order, or on several together at the same time.

To become the best people we can be,
and because good people make good relationships,
it is essential that we:

1. Work at developing our own level of emotional maturity.

2. Learn to deal with anxiety and the sense of emotional threat that inspires it by becoming calmer and a more solid self.

3. Continue to learn to know ourselves and how we actually behave in relation to others, and to be responsible for ourselves.

4. Focus on our own personal goals rather than focusing on others and what they may or may not be doing or what they may or may not want from/for us.

5. Approach important situations with more objective thinking rather than only relying on our feelings.

6. Develop the principles we want to live by and affirm them in our actions, particularly at critical points in life.

How do you want to live your life?

Our understanding of goodness and of what is important in relationships, that is, our values, will inevitably arise out of our set of beliefs about the nature of reality and the philosophical or religious or spiritual basis of our lives. In my work as a therapist, I attempted to help people think through their beliefs and values and what they wanted to base their lives on. In many different ways (but rarely in these specific words) I would ask them, "What is your understanding of goodness? What values do you want to exemplify in your own life? How do you want to live your life in relationship to others?"

Emotional maturity allows us to consistently adhere to our personal principles of goodness. In my own framework of belief, these would be principles such as integrity, loyalty, trustworthiness, honesty, responsibility, justice, faithfulness, respect, generosity, self-control, courage, fairness, concern, and consideration for others. Most therapists would not use these sorts of words with clients, and I rarely introduced them. As I asked clients what was important to them, however, they inevitably began to identify these kinds of qualities as important values in their lives. The challenge was how to consistently live up to them and fulfill them in their relationships.

No doubt most of us would profess a belief in important values like those I listed above. Like most everyone else, my clients were stronger in some areas and weaker in others. This is where emotional maturity comes in. As we work on our level of maturity, we get better at consistently doing what we profess, which improves our relationships. With greater maturity we can better live according to the values we profess.

> Being able to say, "I love you," to your partner is one thing. But being able to *be* loving when the level of tension or anxiety increases in a relationship . . . is another thing entirely.

Like us, Jane Austen's heroes are not perfect, but each one of them wants to be better. Austen shows us how each one has challenges and character flaws to overcome. They seek to grow through the difficult life and relationship situations they face. Part of the joy of reading Austen is watching this growth and seeing her protagonists become stronger and better people. Watching Elizabeth Bennet discover, think through, and deal with her own pride and prejudice, rather than just focusing on Darcy's shortcomings (as she had done), is a powerful experience that leads us to think about ourselves. She learned to be humbler, more tolerant, and not so quick to judge. Part of what I enjoyed as a therapist was watching my clients grow around these kinds of issues.

Being able to say, "I love you," to your partner is one thing. But being able to *be* loving when the level of tension or anxiety increases in a relationship, like when your partner is being critical of you, is another thing entirely. The higher the level of anxiety, the less likely good, loving behavior will be present. It is relatively easy for most of us to behave well when things are going our way; when our partner or family or friends are happy with us and we feel calm. But it is not so easy when things get difficult.

Close relationships are rarely consistently calm and easy. The test for goodness is whether people will behave well when they may feel significant anxiety or uneasiness or a sense of personal threat. Will they behave well when they may be tempted to abandon principle for expediency, or will they automatically react and attack back when feeling attacked and when their love and concern for the other is severely tested? This is what I mean by *being* good.

Courage and compromise

Anxiety in life and relationships tempts us to compromise our professed principles as to how we want to be. A sense of safety and well-being, achieved by reducing the immediate anxiety, can become more important than living up to our values. We choose emotional or physical security over principle. Some of my bravest clients were those who had a higher degree of anxiety than most but who were able to avoid being sidetracked by it. They set their goals in life for how they wanted to be and worked toward achieving them. Claiming their own courage, they did not let their anxiety get in the way.

Judy, a forty-year-old single client, felt intense anxiety in relation to her boss. His criticism sent feelings of terror through her. This sensitivity to what she considered the emotional threat of criticism had kept her from dating men as well. When she came in for therapy, she was having frequent panic attacks at work. Often her boss's criticisms of her work were wrong, but she would conform to what he wanted rather than stand up for what she knew to be correct. She otherwise enjoyed her job and the people she worked with and did not want to just quit.

First, she learned some strategies for calming herself down (#2) when she felt the panic begin to build. Developing a greater level of calmness is a critical component of dealing with anxiety. There is a large literature on dealing with stress, and most of it is also useful for dealing with the closely related experience of anxiety. Eventually Judy decided to go against her anxiety, even though she still experienced it to some degree, and live by what she believed to be correct (#6). She carefully thought through (#5) just what was happening in specific scenarios with her boss, and how she made herself anxious. She took note of facial expressions and tones of voice that had the most impact on her and thought about how she could modify her response. Then she developed goals for how she wanted to behave (#4), even if it meant getting fired due to her boss's unreasonableness.

As she worked at doing this, making good headway and getting the negative reaction she had feared from him, he was suddenly fired. His boss had also taken note of her boss's "pigheaded" style and decided not to take

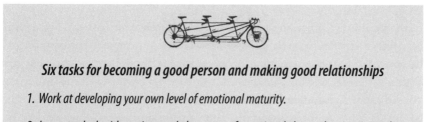

Six tasks for becoming a good person and making good relationships

1. Work at developing your own level of emotional maturity.

2. Learn to deal with anxiety and the sense of emotional threat that inspires it by becoming calmer and a more solid self.

3. Continue to learn to know yourself and how you actually behave in relation to others, and to be responsible for yourself.

4. Focus on your own personal goals rather than focusing on others and what they may or may not be doing or what they may or may not want from/for you.

5. Approach important situations with more objective thinking rather than only relying on your feelings.

6. Develop the principles you want to live by and affirm them in your actions, particularly at critical points in life.

it anymore. She came in to see me in great relief. I said to her, "That's too bad. Who are you going to get to practice being a self (#2) with now?" She got it and we laughed. We assumed she would indeed have many more opportunities for this practice.

Her anxiety was not really about her boss. It was about her and her family life, and this became the focus of her therapy. She made visits home and was able to better observe herself in the context of family (#3) and how, in certain circumstances, she became anxious. She did not look just at her family's behavior and what made them anxious and reactive, but at how she felt and behaved with them when they became anxious. Her new boss continued to provide some occasion for experiencing anxiety, and as she got better with her family, she could do the same with him at work. Eventually she was able to feel much less anxious or intimidated by either her family members or her boss. She was able to be a more solid self with them. Unlike her old boss, her new boss began to value her opinion. The last I heard she had also become involved in a relationship with a man.

Standing up for your values versus craving acceptance

Some people are quite anxious about being accepted by others. For example, Jim, a high school student who was the son of a client, wanted to be included in a particular group of guys. He thought it might raise his status at school and in the eyes of a girl he was interested in. But these guys "dissed" a good friend of his and laughed at him. The young man had to decide what he believed about this and whom he really wanted to be friends with. If he stood up for his friend, the guys might reject him. If he attacked them and told them they were wrong, they would probably attack him in return. Should he compromise his values and beliefs and go along with their jokes in order to be accepted by this group?

He had to do a lot of thinking (#5) about this situation and his conflicting feelings. He told his father (my client), and we talked about how he (the father) could be of help. He was able to help his son, not by telling him what to do, but just by asking questions. This is part of what I had been doing with him in therapy around his own issues. He was able to stay neutral about what his son should do, and his questions helped his son to think through his own beliefs (#5, #6). The questions allowed the son to think more clearly and to be less anxious. As a result, he wondered if he really wanted to be connected with the group of guys.

As he stopped pursuing the goal of joining their group, a couple of the guys he liked asked him why he wasn't coming around so much. He didn't want to make a scene but said that he was having difficulty with their making fun of his friend (#2). They responded, "Cool, good for you." He didn't join the group, but he did feel a new sense of respect coming from them whenever he bumped into them. He was happy that he hadn't compromised his principles (#6).

I didn't know the group of guys involved, but it would be reasonable to assume that there was a certain amount of unrecognized anxiety in their group, normal in most any teen group. They dealt with this by making fun of others. If asked individually, they probably knew this was not a good thing to do. But as a group they may have said, "Hey, that guy is such a nerd. There are too many jerks like him in the world."

We can often be faced with situations like this young man's. He was able to develop a more solid sense of himself (#2) by thinking through (#5) his concerns and standing up for his beliefs (#6). He did not let his anxiety about acceptance undercut his living a more principled life. It was a struggle for him; it was not easy. And he had to do it without reacting to the group of guys (#3) and attacking them for their "shallowness." He ended up feeling better about himself. And the father, my client, developed a new sense of respect for his son. Of course, their relationship improved as well.

This young man did not distance from the group of guys out of anxiety (#2). If he had been anxious, he would have joined the group and gone along with its ethos of criticizing others, or he would have attacked and criticized the group, or he would have hidden from and avoided the group. In contrast, when some members asked him why he wasn't coming around, he was able to say clearly and openly, without attacking them, what his difficulty was (#2). This being a more solid self took courage and it was not comfortable for him, but he was glad he did it. He found an inner sense of comfort in the midst of his anxiety by taking time to think through for himself the principles he wanted to live by (#6).

> Becoming a more solid self and developing principles by which to live our lives is a major goal in life.

Being a solid self and approval

Becoming a more solid self and developing principles by which to live our lives is a major goal in life. Anne Elliot in *Persuasion* is probably the most emotionally mature of Austen's six heroes, but she also has to work hard at becoming a stronger self. Lady Russell became an important mother figure for Anne after her mother died. She had been Anne's mother's best friend. Lady Russell disapproves of Captain Wentworth and his friends because they are not of the right class. Nine years earlier, she had persuaded Anne as a young woman to break off her engagement to him. However, Anne is still in love with him and enjoys his friends. Anne has to risk Lady Russell's deep disapproval in order to be the person she wants to be.

What her father and sister think of her is less important to Anne, so she is not anxious about their reaction to her love interest. But she has to be willing to let go of Lady Russell's support and friendship as she moves toward Captain Wentworth. At this point in the story, Captain Wentworth appears to be more interested in Louisa Musgrove than in Anne. In chapter 13 we can see Anne's anxiety in her encounter with Lady Russell in the resort town of Bath. They begin by discussing Louisa's near-fatal accident at Lyme Regis. Then they ease into recognition of Captain Wentworth's presence in town.

> There was a little awkwardness at first in their discourse on another subject. They must speak of the accident at Lyme. Lady Russell had not been arrived five minutes the day before, when a full account of the whole had burst on her; but still it must be talked of . . . and Captain Wentworth's name must be mentioned by both. Anne was conscious of not doing it so well as Lady Russell. She could not speak the name, and look straight forward to Lady Russell's eye, till she had adopted the expedient of telling her briefly what she thought of the attachment between him and Louisa. When this was told, his name distressed her no longer.

If we wait for permission and approval from important others before we do what makes sense to us, we will never become our own true selves (#2). In Anne's case, she eventually finds the courage to be more open (#4) with Lady Russell, who eventually shows her own growing maturity and adjusts her own attitudes. She learns to accept Captain Wentworth and does not break off her relationship with Anne, as Anne had feared. At important junctures, we must be willing to undergo such losses if we are to develop our own selves. Anne's courage is shown in being willing to endure that loss.

One young client, Dean, was getting married. I had done some pre-marital work with him and his fiancée, Bobbie, which led them both to do some family-of-origin work. In the course of his work, Dean discovered an aunt, uncle, and some cousins whom his parents had been cut off from even before he was born. He had not really heard anything about them before this. He visited them and decided he wanted to invite them to his wedding. When his mother heard about this, she said he "absolutely must not do it." He tried to find out more about why she was against it, but could only discover that his mother's fight with her sister had something to do with their parents. She had not had contact with her sister for more than thirty years and never wanted to see her again. She was adamant about this.

> When people have the realization that they do not have to be victims of other people's wants and demands, it is a gift of emotional freedom.

We talked about what he was going to do. Dean didn't know how, but he believed the cutoff between the sisters had something to do with his own family experience, and he was eager to overcome this cutoff for himself. He decided with his fiancée that it was their wedding and the guest list was their right. He told his mother that he was inviting this missing part of the family. She said, speaking for her husband as well, "Then we are not coming to your wedding." He said, "That makes me very sad, Mother. I really do want you to come, and I will feel quite bad if you don't. I want you to join in with my happiness and be a part of this new family we are creating. But I am inviting my aunt, uncle, and cousins. That is also important to me."

He stood by his decision, and right through the day before the wedding, at the rehearsal dinner, his mother refused to come if her sister's family came. He did not react to his mother's displeasure with him. She said it was his fault that she was not coming. He did not argue with her about this or try to convince her she was wrong, and he did not try to blame her for "ruining" the wedding. He just kept telling her that it was important to him that she and his father come to the wedding. She kept saying no, but on the day of the wedding, both mother and father attended the ceremony and the reception afterward. The two sisters were civil toward each other and did speak. Only over time did he begin to get the full story as he talked with each of them, asking questions that simply invited them to rethink the nature of their feud. They began to come to family get-togethers that he and Bobbie hosted in their new house. Eventually they began to act as if there had been no fight at all. He thought each was genuinely glad to have her sister back as a friend. He also felt a reduced level of emotional intensity coming at him from his mother. Their relationship improved as well. I am sure the work he did also benefited his marriage.

Freedom to change

When people have the realization that they do not have to be victims of other people's wants and demands, it is a gift of emotional freedom. To blame others for how we live is to put others in charge of our lives: we are then their victims; we think we are the way we are because of others. If this were true, it would mean that we couldn't change and be happier until they changed. Believing this usually takes us down a road of futility and frustration in relationships. If Dean had caved in to his mother, he probably would have built resentment toward her, thinking, wrongly, "She is still running my life." To take responsibility for ourselves is to claim the freedom to take charge of our own lives and of our response to the circumstances of our lives. We do not have to be victims of the wishes, or wants, or goals, or negligence, or bad behavior of other people.

When John came in for therapy after his wife divorced him, he was a pretty miserable person. His friends had insisted that he needed to talk with someone because they were concerned about him. He described himself as a "hopeless romantic" and said that he still loved his wife and couldn't face life without her. He believed he had no choice; it was his fate. Only gradually did he begin to see that he could choose the way he looked at the relationship.

I suspected that he was not facing the facts of his situation and suggested that he invite his former wife to come in with him for a session. I wanted to hear what she said about the marriage. She agreed to come with him to one session, during which she confessed to having been involved with another man while still married to John. He was, of course, shocked to learn this. Now she and the other man were planning to marry. In addition, she said that her experience with John in the marriage was difficult for her because he was "like a puppy dog that didn't have a life of his own." Everything in his life seemed to focus around her, and she just wanted to get away from him. If she was happy with him, he was ecstatic, and if not, then he was in the dumps. She felt responsible for everything about his life and she couldn't take it. She didn't know how else to deal with him except to distance and leave the marriage.

After this very tough session, John and I talked about how he needed to "get a life." These were his words. This became his first goal (#4). He had a good job but he thought he could upgrade his work skills. He started a night school MBA course and eventually got the degree. We talked about what personal interests he might pursue. He liked photography. He joined a local club that was quite active with both meetings and outings.

Eventually, as John began to date again, we were able to look at his repeated pattern of dependency. We traced it back to his family experience and he started making family visits, doing some good family work. He read my book *Family Ties That Bind*, and that became our model for his work. He was amazingly good at meeting women and getting dates, but these relationships didn't progress very far because the women would shy away from his dependent intensity. He slowly began to take responsibility for his own experience and mood (#3) and became more aware of how his anxiety could affect him (#2) and less affected by what he thought were the reactions of the women he was dating (#4). He became more thought-ful about how he wanted to be with them (#5) rather than fearing what he thought they thought of him.

It was challenging work for him, but he got much better at connecting with women in a more secure and confident way, feeling freer to be himself (#2) and less anxious about what others thought of him. Whenever he got somewhat anxious, he was tempted to focus on the partner and how she was with him, but he made progress as he kept reminding himself what he was doing. As several relationships did not work out, he was able, more and more, to look just at his part separate from whatever the women brought to the relationship.

He terminated therapy, saying he knew what he needed to do; I agreed with him, although I still had trouble imagining John taking a principled stand with a woman he loved. Two years later he called to say he was married and he wanted to come in with his wife to talk about how things were going. In that one interview, it was clear to me that he was doing much better and being more realistic about the responsibility tangle. His wife said she was enjoying her life with John, but this was hard for me to assess in one session.

It did become clear to me that John wanted this interview partly because of his dependence on my opinion—had he indeed done well? On the surface I stayed neutral and kept turning his implied question ("Aren't I doing well?") back to him, asking him for evidence of his belief that he was doing better. But I'm sure he saw that I was pleased with his progress, so he and I had our own little responsibility tangle going on! This is an endemic issue for most therapists stemming from our own lack of maturity. When we are no longer invested in whether our clients do well or not, they will do best because then their efforts are truly for themselves, not for us. This encounter made clear to me that there was room for improvement in my own emotional maturity.

> In taking responsibility for self, we need also to do what we can to take responsibility for the consequences of our actions.

Responsibility to others

This kind of responsibility tangle often leaves us feeling responsible for others, or it leaves them thinking they are responsible for us. Maybe John wanted to reassure me that I had done a good job as a therapist; maybe I wanted that from him. Sorting out the responsibility tangle and clarifying who is responsible for what does not mean that we have no responsibilities in relation to others. While I was not responsible for how well John did (that was his responsibility), I was responsible to be the best therapist I could be with him. I think I partly failed him in that regard. I had a responsibility *to* him that I might have managed better if I had felt less responsible *for* him.

In more serious ways, when one's own behavior creates problems and unhappiness for others, it is time to take responsibility for one's actions or lack of action. A good example of this is when Darcy (*Pride and Prejudice*), out of a prideful regard for protecting his family's privacy and his own stature in the eyes of others, fails to warn Elizabeth and her family about Wickham's character and past behavior in relation to Darcy's younger sister. After Wickham has eloped with Lydia, he sees how he is responsible for not warning the family. He is not responsible for Lydia's or Wickham's behavior, but he sees how he helped to contribute to the situation by not providing relevant information to Elizabeth, Lydia, and their family. Recognizing this, he then does what he can to remedy the situation. A letter from her Aunt Gardiner, in chapter 52, tells Elizabeth how Darcy did this.

> On the very day of my coming home from Longbourn, your uncle had a most unexpected visitor. Mr. Darcy called, and was shut up with him several hours. It was all over before I arrived; so my curiosity was not so dreadfully racked as *yours* seems to have been. He came to tell Mr. Gardiner that he had found out where your sister and Mr. Wickham were, and that he had seen and talked with them both; Wickham repeatedly, Lydia once. From what I can collect, he left Derbyshire only one day after ourselves, and came to town with the resolution of hunting for them. The motive professed was his conviction of its being owing to himself that Wickham's worthlessness had not been so well known as to make it impossible for any young woman of character to love or confide in him. He generously imputed the whole to his mistaken pride, and confessed that he had before thought it beneath him to lay his private actions open to the world. His character was to speak for itself. He called it, therefore, his duty to step forward, and endeavour to remedy an evil which had been brought on by himself.

In taking responsibility for self, we need also to do what we can to take responsibility for the consequences of our actions. Darcy overcomes his own pride and hidden shame by being more open about how Wickham had managed to nearly seduce his own younger sister. This, plus other acts by him, leads Elizabeth to reconsider her words and behavior toward him and to take more responsibility for her own actions.

> They owed the restoration of Lydia, her character, every thing, to him. Oh! how heartily did she grieve over every ungracious sensation she had ever encouraged, every saucy speech she had ever directed towards him. For herself she was humbled; but she was

proud of him. Proud that in a cause of compassion and honour, he had been able to get the better of himself. She read over her aunt's commendation of him again and again.

Learning to take this kind of responsibility for ourselves and for our own actions requires that we pay a great deal of attention to our own behavior and how we want to be, rather than focusing on how others are behaving and how we want them to be. Darcy overcame his sense of shame and his fear of how others saw him and his family. "His mistaken pride" had caused him to behave irresponsibly toward others. Once he realized this, he was able to become a better person in his relationships with others and act out of "compassion and honour."

This kind of stance takes courage. It requires the willingness to evaluate our own behavior and to recognize our mistakes. It is not easy. Elizabeth found it humiliating to have been so wrong about both Darcy and Wickham. Her pride in what she thinks of as her good judgment about others gets in the way of being wise. Her lack of wisdom, of true good judgment, generosity, and lack of humility, means she has not behaved justly toward Darcy. She reflects on her "unjust accusations" against him. Good relationships require that we exercise the virtue of "justice" toward others.

Elizabeth is committed to being a good person and becoming more emotionally mature. In this case, that means she has to be willing to reevaluate her snap judgments about people. This requires facing the truth about herself as well as others. Every effort we make toward becoming better people will not only make us happier but also improve our relationships with others. I hope the examples from my clinical practice and from Jane Austen have demonstrated the wisdom of making these efforts. I hope, too, that you have had similar experiences in your own life.

⟨ Thirteen ⟩

A Final Example
from Jane Austen

Each one of Jane Austen's heroes demonstrates the principles I am talking about in this book. On the road to greater emotional maturity, they become more solid selves in relation to family, friends, and lovers. Getting the approval of others is not their primary goal, nor is winning the men they love. They simply want to be good people in their relationships with those they care about. Their striving to be so is truly heroic, which is why we admire them.

In this last chapter I want to offer a final, extended example from Austen's *Emma*. In a lengthy passage, Austen is specific about what we need to do to be more emotionally mature. She embodies her thoughts in one of the delightful interactions between Mr. Knightley and Emma. Through much of the novel he acts as her mentor since her mother is dead and her somewhat self-centered father is useless as a guide in living a good life. Mr. Knightley has played this role for her for many years, and she values him as a very good friend with whom she rather delights in debating various issues and taking positions contrary to his. She has not yet realized that she might be in love with him or that he might be in love with her.

The following passage is from chapter 18 of *Emma*. In it, Mr. Knightley and Emma are discussing Frank Churchill, a young man who has not yet appeared upon the scene. Frank is known of by many people in town and some have speculated that he might be a good partner in marriage for Emma. He is handsome, lively, has a good personality, and is potentially wealthy. Emma knows of the speculation and is waiting to see for herself. Mr. Knightley also knows of this speculation, and he, of course, has his own personal reasons for wanting to convince Emma that Frank is not the most honorable person.

Frank is Mr. Weston's son from a previous marriage. Mr. Weston is a well-respected man in town who lost his first wife shortly after the birth of their son. Mr. Weston did not think he could raise a child on his own, so his dead wife's sister and her husband agreed to raise him. Since death of the mother in childbirth was a common enough experience, it was not unusual for relatives to take responsibility for the child.

Mr. and Mrs. Churchill, who did not have children of their own, became Frank's adopted parents, even though they were actually his aunt and uncle. Frank grew up using their last name as his own. It was always known to Frank that Mr. Weston was his father. Frank became very important to Mrs. Churchill in particular. Out of her anxiety and fear of losing him back to Mr. Weston, she became a possessive and controlling mother.

This discussion between Mr. Knightley and Emma is precipitated by Mr. Weston's remarriage. He married Emma's governess, Miss Taylor. It would have been appropriate for Frank to come to the town of Highbury to meet her and to congratulate the couple. But Frank had delayed his coming for some time now and sent letters to his father (who has relayed their content to his friends) explaining why it was not yet possible for him to come. It was obvious to most people that the problem in his coming was his adopted mother, Mrs. Churchill. Her anxiety or emotional insecurity leads her to use money as a way to control his attachment to her.

Frank is totally dependent financially on his adopted parents. They are quite wealthy, and at their death he will inherit a significant estate. Until that time he lives on an income they provide for him. It is clear that he so fears upsetting them, Mrs. Churchill in particular, that he regularly bows to their wishes.

In the passage below, Mr. Knightley says that a man of true principle would know how to handle this situation. Even though Mrs. Churchill would resist his self-definition, in the long run she would learn to trust and respect him for acting on principle. Her emotional resistance would give way to appreciation and acceptance, Mr. Knightley says, because she would know Frank was right. Additionally, Frank's act of self-definition would be reassuring to her because he would then be seen as a man of principle; he could be counted on to do the right thing by her. If he failed to act on principle, she

It is within and in relation to our own family that we must first develop and demonstrate our emotional maturity and define a more solid self.

would know, intuitively, that he was untrustworthy, which would likely increase her anxiety.

I like this passage because Austen makes clear that it is within and in relation to our own family that we must first develop and demonstrate our emotional maturity and define a more solid self. If, as young adults, we can do this in the process of leaving home, then we will be more mature people generally in our adult lives. If not, we will carry our emotional immaturity with us into our other adult relationships. Part of why Austen liked English country village life, as compared to city life, is because everyone knew the character of their neighbors and the people they lived with and did business with. If Frank ever moved back to his father's village, there would be some lingering question about his character based on his recent behavior.

What no one yet knows (it is a big secret) is that Frank is secretly engaged to Jane Fairfax. Jane is an orphan who is related to her poor aunt (Mrs. Bates) in the village and has no money of her own. She was raised by another adoptive couple, friends of her dead parents, who live elsewhere. She and Frank met at a seaside resort and quickly struck up a love relationship that led to his proposal to her. But he is waiting for the right moment to break this news to Mrs. Churchill, who, he knows, will be angry and might possibly cut him off financially if he were to marry Jane. As a result, when he does come to town, he behaves badly in relation to Jane, since he wants to keep their engagement a secret. He flirts with Emma and shows little interest in Jane. This only further affirms that Frank is not an honorable man.

What makes the following dialogue so true to life is that Emma, taking a more accepting stance of Frank's behavior in relation to visiting his father, and how he deals with Mrs. Churchill, says that it is easy for Mr. Knightley to take the position he does. She says he is used to being in charge of his own life and defining himself as he wishes. Emma has more sympathy for the difficulties faced by Frank in relation to his family. She can identify with the slow development of his emotional maturity within such a family as his. While, on the one hand, Emma appears to have her own father wrapped around her little finger, she is, in fact, very sensitive to his dependency on her, and much of her life is governed by his wants and wishes, just as Frank's is by Mrs. Churchill's wants and wishes. As we see later in the story, her father's dependency governs aspects of her own marriage.

Although Mr. Knightley's somewhat self-righteous and passionate argument stems partly out of his own anxious jealousy that Emma may be entertaining the idea of falling in love with Frank, he still makes valid points about character and emotional maturity. He clearly identifies the need to define a self within one's family as the path to emotional maturity. And Emma clearly outlines what makes such a principled position difficult to achieve within family relationships. They debate the struggle of developing a mature, solid self in family life, and how anxiety over acceptance, money, and having a dependable income from his adopted parents interferes with Frank's being more grown up. In this passage Austen does an incredible job of looking at both sides of the issue. Mr. Knightley says:

"There is one thing, Emma, which a man can always do, if he chuses, and that is, his duty; not by manoeuvring and finessing, but by vigour and resolution. It is Frank Churchill's duty to pay this attention to his father. . . . A man who felt rightly would say at once, simply and resolutely, to Mrs. Churchill—'Every sacrifice of mere pleasure you will always find me ready to make to your convenience; but I must go and see my father immediately. I know he would be hurt by my failing in such a mark of respect to him on the present occasion. I shall, therefore, set off to-morrow.'—If he would say so to her at once, in the tone of decision becoming a man, there would be no opposition made to his going."

"No," said Emma, laughing; "but perhaps there might be some made to his coming back again. Such language for a young man entirely dependent, to use!—Nobody but you, Mr. Knightley, would imagine it possible. But you have not an idea of what is requisite in situations directly opposite to your own. Mr. Frank Churchill to be making such a speech as that to the uncle and aunt, who have brought him up, and are to provide for him!—Standing up in the middle of the room, I suppose, and speaking as loud as he could!—How can you imagine such conduct practicable?"

"Depend upon it, Emma, a sensible man would find no difficulty in it. He would feel himself in the right; and the declaration—made, of course, as a man of sense would make it, in a proper manner—would do him more good, raise him higher, fix his interest stronger with the people he depended on, than all that a line of shifts and expedients can ever do. Respect would be added to affection. They would feel that they could trust him; that the nephew who had done rightly by his father, would do rightly by them; for they know, as well as he does, as well as all the world must know, that he ought to pay this visit to his father; and while meanly exerting their power to delay it, are in their hearts not thinking the better of him for submitting to their whims. Respect for right conduct is felt by every body. If he would act in this sort of manner, on principle, consistently, regularly, their little minds would bend to his."

"I rather doubt that. You are very fond of bending little minds; but where little minds belong to rich people in authority, I think they have a knack of swelling out, till they are quite as unmanageable as great ones. I can imagine, that if you, as you are, Mr. Knightley, were to be transported and placed all at once in Mr. Frank Churchill's situation, you would be able to say and do just what you have been recommending for him; and it might have a very good effect. The Churchills might not have a word to say in return; but then, you would have no habits of early obedience and long observance to break through. To him who has, it might not be so easy to burst forth at once into perfect independence, and set all their claims on his gratitude and regard at nought. He may have as strong a sense of what would be right, as you can have, without being so equal, under particular circumstances, to act up to it."

"Then it would not be so strong a sense. If it failed to produce equal exertion, it could not be an equal conviction."

"Oh, the difference of situation and habit! I wish you would try to understand what an amiable young man may be likely to feel in directly opposing those, whom as child and boy he has been looking up to all his life."

"Our amiable young man is a very weak young man, if this be the first occasion of his carrying through a resolution to do right against the will of others. It ought to have been a habit with him by this time, of following his duty, instead of consulting expediency. I can allow for the fears of the child, but not of the man. As he became rational, he ought to have roused himself and shaken off all that was unworthy in their authority. He ought to have opposed the first attempt on their side to make him slight his father. Had he begun as he ought, there would have been no difficulty now."

"We shall never agree about him," cried Emma; "but that is nothing extraordinary. I have not the least idea of his being a weak young man: I feel sure that he is not. Mr. Weston would not be blind to folly, though in his own son; but he is very likely to have a more yielding, complying, mild disposition than would suit your notions of man's perfection. I dare say he has; and though it may cut him off from some advantages, it will secure him many others."

"Yes; all the advantages of sitting still when he ought to move, and of leading a life of mere idle pleasure, and fancying himself extremely expert in finding excuses for it. He can sit down and write a fine flourishing letter, full of professions and falsehoods, and persuade himself that he has hit upon the very best method in the world of preserving peace at home and preventing his father's having any right to complain. His letters disgust me."

"Your feelings are singular. They seem to satisfy every body else."

To the extent that we have all had difficulty nonreactively defining ourselves to our parents and within our families, we will find ourselves taking Emma's side in this debate and agreeing with her about the difficulty of doing what Mr. Knightley says should be done. To the extent that we have been able to do what he proposes, we will see the correctness and truth of his position.

Note that as they debate the degree to which Frank is an emotionally mature, solid self (versus being "a weak young man"), Emma attempts to define herself in relation to Mr. Knightley, her mentor and as-yet unknown lover. She is comfortable taking a position contrary to his, but she does not yet know herself well enough to be completely open with him. In fact, she probably agrees with Mr. Knightley more than she allows. As the truth about Frank begins to emerge, she takes responsibility for her inability to see it. She eventually decides that Frank Churchill is not a worthy young man and is too full of dissimulation. However, getting to know herself better is the primary task for Emma in the novel. She has many feeling-driven fantasies about herself and others that need some solid, thoughtful discovery of facts to correct.

Frank Churchill did eventually come to pay his respects and to congratulate his father and his new wife, but he managed it through "manoeuvring and finessing," rather than by "vigour and resolution" with the Churchills. And he eventually became freer to do as he wished as a result of Mrs. Churchill's sudden death. We can be sure, however, that Frank has not really changed. Her death did not change him; it just released him from that particular constraint.

Until Frank works at being a more emotionally mature person, he will continue to find people whom he will think of as constricting him and holding him back from doing what he wants. And he will have to "maneuver and finesse" rather than being more straightforward. He will think of others as in charge of him and feel like their victim. Surely he will think of his eventual wife, Jane Fairfax, in this way.

Unless Frank changes, his marriage to Jane will not be a happy one. A niece of Austen's once asked her what will become of Jane. Austen replied that Jane would die not too many years after her marriage to Frank. She indicated that this death would be the result of a somewhat frail constitution. Maybe it would also result from a less-than-happy marriage and a broken heart.

Jane's story goes with Frank's story, and it is a sad one. She is a highly likable person, and it is especially sad, I think, that she and Emma could not be friends. Due to her secret relationship with Frank, Jane became reserved and kept her distance from people. She was not open and spontaneous because she had to stay guarded. This was hard on her and she became depressed. Finally she gave up on Frank and decided that she would have to do the thing she had deeply dreaded, which was to break off the engagement and practically sell herself into servitude by becoming a governess. This act of self-definition shook up Frank and gave him the resolve to win her back and to make their engagement open, come whatever may happen with Mrs. Churchill. Would he actually have done it? We don't know because her sudden death releases him from having to make this choice.

In their story, Austen shows, as I have argued in this book, that virtue and happiness go hand in hand. In her novels she shows us over and over again what it takes to become a person of good character or, as I would say, an emotionally mature person. It is my hope that this book has helped you understand what is required for you to become your own best person. If you would like to pursue the subject further, there is no better way to do so than to read more Jane Austen.

Questions for Individual and Group Reflection

Chapter 1

1. The author states that it is not the relationship itself but the behavior of those in the relationship that is the problem in failed relationships. Do you agree? Why or why not?
2. What is the difference between (1) complaining, "My relationship doesn't work," and (2) confessing, "Perhaps it's my attitudes and behavior in the relationship that don't work"?
3. What does the expression "Character is destiny" mean to you? Give some examples that illustrate your understanding. Do you agree with the author that character can be changed (and therefore so can our destiny) when we are adults? Explain.
4. In what ways has your family of origin contributed to your level of emotional maturity or emotional reactivity? Do you sense a need for greater emotional maturity in your life? Explain.

Chapter 2

1. The author lists "moral attitudes" such as gratitude, altruism, forgiveness, and compassion as principles of living (or values) that should impact our behavior in relationships. Reflect on how these values do (or do not) inform the way you relate to others.
2. What other principles of living or values have you consciously chosen that guide your behavior in life generally and particularly in your relationships? Why did you choose them?
3. How would you define a "good person"?
4. In what ways do you (or do you not) think that "good" people have better, happier, more meaningful relationships?

Chapter 3

1. In what ways does our culture promote cynicism with respect to the values of virtue and goodness? Do you share this cynicism? Why or why not?
2. In what ways do your faith commitments and faith community assist you and others (especially children) in developing a strong character based on strong virtues?
3. Are feelings a good measure of a relationship? Why or why not? What might be healthy and productive ways of expressing your feelings in a close relationship?
4. What seems more important to you: the way you feel about your partner or the way you behave toward your partner? Why? How can you change the focus from personal feelings to personal behavior?

Chapter 4

1. Life in the modern world is rife with anxieties. Make a list of all that you are anxious about. Reflect on how these anxieties impact your feelings and shape your behavior.
2. In what ways (if any) have your anxieties led you to betray your values by causing behavior that violates your chosen principles for living?
3. Jesus said that we are to love others as we love ourselves. What does it mean to you to love yourself? How does one balance love of self and love of the other?
4. Reflect on the many ways people "hide" from each other in relationships. What are your favorite ways of hiding? What would you need to do to stop hiding?

Chapter 5

1. The author writes that "change nearly always evokes some anxiety because it introduces us to the uncertainties of a new situation." How do you typically respond to change? How does the experience of change impact your behavior in relationships?
2. What does the author's expression "solid self" mean to you?
3. Do you see yourself as a solid self? Explain. How might you work on becoming a more solid self?

4. Think of people in your life whom you experience as a "less anxious presence." What characteristics do they demonstrate in times of conflict or crisis?

Chapter 6

1. What (at the present moment) is your definition of happiness? Do you consider yourself a happy person? Why or why not?
2. Do you agree that in dealing with an unhappy relationship, an individual's focus should be on himself or herself and not the other? Why or why not?
3. In what ways can a lack of self-knowledge lead to unhappy relationships? What strategies might one follow in becoming more objective about himself or herself?
4. Make lists of (1) your goals, (2) your beliefs, (3) your values, and (4) how you behave in relationships. Reflect on the lists. What connections do you see between them? What do they tell you about yourself? Any changes suggested?

Chapter 7

1. According to the author, "Being responsible for self includes being able to think and make judgments for ourselves." As you reflect on your relationships, do you see yourself as someone who mostly takes responsibility for self or who mostly defers to others to think for you and make judgments for you?
2. In what ways did your parents' sense (or lack of sense) of responsibility for self encourage or impede the development of your own sense of responsibility for self? Are you happy with your current level of responsibility for self? Why or why not?
3. Reflect on how you act and react in relationships. Do you see in yourself any signs of what the author calls "learned helplessness" (the belief that you are powerless to change your circumstances)? Explain.
4. What is your understanding of the role of willpower in shaping the way we behave in relationships?

Chapter 8

1. Make a list of your relationship goals; that is, a list of the character traits you want to express in your relationships. What, if anything, hinders your realization of these goals?
2. Give examples of the difference between setting goals for your own behavior in a relationship and setting goals for your partner.
3. Reflect on these questions: How do others make me happy? How do I make others happy? Are these good questions to ask with respect to your relationships? Why or why not?
4. How would you describe the difference between "self-focus" and "selfish focus"? What are the likely consequences of self-focus in a relationship? What are the likely consequences of selfish focus in a relationship?

Chapter 9

1. Make a list of your significant relationships—family, friends, colleagues. For each relationship, list your expectations of the other. Make a list of the expectations you have of yourself in each relationship. Reflect on all of these expectations. Do they seem reasonable? Why or why not?
2. What expectations do you feel others have of you in your most significant relationships? Do they seem reasonable? Are there any you need to have clarified or negotiated?
3. In what ways (if any) do other people and/or circumstances set the emotional tone of your life? Who should be setting the emotional tone of your life?
4. Do you tend to make judgments and take action on the basis of your feelings, or do you tend to make judgments and take action on the basis of thoughtful reflection on more objective facts and behaviors? Explain.

Chapter 10

1. What, if any, emotional rights do you think you have vis-à-vis other people that you expect them to honor by behaving in ways that produce in you the feelings you have a "right" to?
2. Reflect on what it would be like to take full responsibility for your own feelings and behavior.

3. Write a few paragraphs or a few pages answering these questions: What kind of a person do I want to be? How do I want to live my life? Why do I think this way? What do I need to do to be more authentic; to be the author of my life?

4. Make a list of the role models, the "heroes of goodness" you have known and who inspire you. What are the character traits or qualities they demonstrate that you most value? Seek them out, if possible, and interview them; find out how they became the way they are, how they integrate their values and beliefs into their relationships.

Chapter 11

1. The fear of rejection or of losing a relationship can exert a powerful force working against an individual's taking a principled stand. What might be reasons to take the stand in spite of such fear—even if the fear is realized?

2. In emotional systems (such as families or work relationships) taking a principled stand can invite "punishment" or "inducements" from members of the system who don't want change. Have you ever experienced punishment or inducements to get you to abandon a principled stand and "go along"? If so, what were the consequences?

3. In what ways might taking a principled stand express commitment both to self and to the relationship?

4. Principled differences usually require noncooperation with family, friends, or colleagues who think and desire differently. What emotional tone should inform the noncooperation of those who find it necessary to take a principled stand in important relationships? Why?

Chapter 12

1. Read through and reflect on, in the light of your own experience, the author's "Six Tasks for Becoming a Good Person and Making Good Relationships":

   1. Work at developing your own level of emotional maturity.

   2. Learn to deal with anxiety and the sense of emotional threat that inspires it by becoming calmer and a more solid self.

3. Continue to learn to know yourself and how you actually behave in relation to others, and to be responsible for yourself.

4. Focus on your own personal goals rather than focusing on others and what they may or may not be doing or what they may or may not want from/for you.

5. Approach important situations with more objective thinking rather than only relying on your feelings.

6. Develop the principles you want to live by and affirm them in your actions, particularly at critical points in life.

2. Which of these six tasks do you consider to be strengths that you could further develop? Explain.
3. Which of these six tasks do you consider to be growth areas that—with some work—you could turn into strengths? Explain.
4. What do you need to do to more fully integrate these six tasks into the way you approach life and relationships?

Chapter 13

1. What are the key insights you have gained about what it means to be an emotionally mature, solid self from reading this book?
2. What key insights have you gained about yourself in general and how you are in relationships in particular from reading this book?
3. Having read this book, do you have a clearer understanding of how you want to live your life? Of how you want to be in relationships? Explain.
4. Having read this book, what are your personal and relationship goals as you move ahead in your life?

☙ FOR FURTHER READING ☙

Bowen, Murray. 1978. *Family Therapy in Clinical Practice*. New York: Jason Aronson.

Butler, Marilyn. 1975. *Jane Austen and the War of Ideas*. Oxford: Clarendon.

Dhatwalia, H. R. 1988. *Familial Relationships in Jane Austen's Novels*. New Delhi: National Book Organization.

Friedman, Edwin H. 1985. *Generation to Generation: Family Process in Church and Synagogue*. New York: Guildford.

Johnson, Claudia. 1988. *Jane Austen: Women, Politics, and the Novel*. Chicago: University of Chicago Press.

Kerr, Michael E., and Murray Bowen. 1988. *Family Evaluation: The Role of Family as an Emotional Unit That Governs Individual Behavior and Development*. New York: Norton.

Richardson, Lois, and Ronald W. Richardson. 1990. *Birth Order and You: How Your Sex and Position in the Family Affects Your Personality and Relationships*. Vancouver: Self-Counsel.

Richardson, Ronald W. 2005. *Becoming a Healthier Pastor: Family Systems Theory and the Pastor's Own Family*. Minneapolis: Augsburg Fortress.

_____. 1996. *Creating a Healthier Church: Family Systems Theory, Leadership, and Congregational Life*. Creative Pastoral Care and Counseling Series. Minneapolis: Fortress Press.

_____. 1984. *Family Ties That Bind: A Self-Help Guide to Change through Family of Origin Therapy*. Vancouver: Self-Counsel.

Ruderman, Anne Crippen. 1995. *The Pleasures of Virtue: Political Thought in the Novels of Jane Austen*. Maryland: Rowman & Littlefield.

Tanner, Tony. 1986. *Jane Austen*. Cambridge: Harvard University Press.

Tomalin, Claire. 1999. *Jane Austen: A Life*. New York: Vintage.